# Guided
# Composition

# Guided Composition

## SECOND EDITION

**Florence Baskoff**

New York University
The American Language Institute

HOUGHTON MIFFLIN COMPANY    BOSTON

Dallas    Geneva, Illinois    Hopewell, New Jersey    Palo Alto

## Acknowledgments

The author and publisher would like to thank the following people for their in-depth reviews of *Guided Composition, First Edition*. Their comments and suggestions were invaluable in preparing the manuscript for this second edition.

Laurie Moody
Passaic County Community College

Frank Pialorsi
University of Arizona

Nanci Phillips
Rio Hondo Community College

Ravi Sheorey
Oklahoma State University

In addition, the author would like to thank her colleagues at the American Language Institute and especially Milton G. Saltzer and Associate Dean L. Steven Zwerling for their support and encouragement.

Illustrations by Glenna Lang.

Student's Edition ISBN: 0-395-34624-X

Instructor's Annotated Edition ISBN: 0-395-34625-8

ABCDEFGHIJ-M-8987654

# TABLE OF CONTENTS

# PREFACE

*To the Student*

The purpose of this book is to teach you how to write in English by giving you ample practice in writing your own compositions, starting with the very first lesson. The book also aims to help you communicate better in writing by giving you a better knowledge of the grammatical structures of the language and by making this a working knowledge through constant application.

The lessons are planned to help you gain both the mechanics (the ability to spell, punctuate, and follow grammatical conventions) and a degree of competency (what to say, how to organize it, and how to say it) in your writing. The topic of the composition is always something that is within your personal experience or knowledge, so you will have "what to say." The model compositions and an outline show you "how to organize it." In addition, the model compositions help you acquire the necessary repertory of words, phrases, and sentences for "how to say it."

By learning to follow the models, you are assured of a minimum number of errors and are less apt to become discouraged. You will soon find that you are gaining more confidence in your writing ability and that you are learning how to write in an organized and understandable manner. The task of writing is made as pleasant as possible.

Each lesson is divided into a number of parts:

## Model Composition

Each model composition uses some particular structure in the English language. The early lessons are simple and then, gradually, they become more complex as you learn how to write. Read and study each model composition carefully. It will show you how to organize your own compositions and it will give you many of the vocabulary words and phrases you may need. Try to read the model composition aloud so that you hear the rhythm and intonation of the words, phrases, and sentences in a connected discourse.

## Vocabulary and Common Expressions

The model is usually followed by a list of new words and expressions used in that composition. Go over the list carefully and make sure you know these words and expressions. You will need some of them in writing your own compositions. Try to answer the questions based on these items. The questions require you to answer in complete sentences using these words and phrases in another context. This will help you understand the new words and remember them.

### Structure

Each lesson has a short explanation of a particular grammatical structure contained in the model composition. There are exercises that follow to give you practice in these structures.

### Activities

Many of the lessons contain activity exercises to be done with a partner or in groups. These activities will help you practice and express your ideas in a peer group as preparation for writing your own individual composition.

### Dictations / Dicto-comps

The dictations and dicto-comps will improve your listening skills at the same time as they give you additional practice in writing in a connected discourse style. In addition, the dicto-comps will give you practice in taking notes and in reconstructing a paragraph based on your aural comprehension and note-taking ability.

### Outline and Composition Writing

The outline at the end of the lesson is the outline of the model composition. It gives you the skeleton organization for the composition you are going to write. You *must* follow this outline and the model when you write your own composition. The outline will organize your composition, and the model composition will give you necessary words, phrases, and structures. You will write about your own ideas, facts, and experience, but you *must* stay within the framework of the outline and the model composition. In some lessons, you will be asked to write your own outline. As you progress, you will be able to write more freely, but always following the outline.

## Handbook

In the back of the book you will find a Short Handbook that will give you additional help in learning how to write compositions and letters and that will assist you in improving your ability to write in different styles.

## Quizzes

In the back of the book you will also find one or two quizzes per lesson based on the model composition. These quizzes will help you check yourself to see if you have really learned the prepositions, verb forms, etc. used in the model composition.

If you follow the model composition and outline and complete the exercises in each lesson, you should have very few errors in your composition. Before long, if you use the book correctly and follow the instructions, you will find that you *can* write in English, and that you can put your grammatical and lexical knowledge to work so that you will be able to communicate better, especially in writing.

Remember, learning how to write takes constant practice. You can do it!

## To the Instructor

*Guided Composition* is a textbook for students of English as a Second or Foreign Language at the beginning through intermediate levels. It is written in the belief that composition writing in connected English paragraph form can be taught starting with the beginning level if proper sequencing is followed. The writing activities in the text are combined with listening, speaking, and reading activities so that all four skills will be reinforced.

For a complete description of the program, please see the Instructor's Annotated Edition.

Aa Bb Cc Dd Ee

Ff Gg Hh Ii Jj Kk

Ll Mm Nn Oo Pp

Qq Rr Ss Tt Uu

Vv Ww Xx Yy Zz

1 2 3 4 5 6 7 8 9 0

# PARAGRAPH FORM

A paragraph is a group of sentences that talks about only one idea. We call this idea *the topic* of the paragraph.

The first line of every paragraph is indented. This means that the first line begins a little further to the right than the other lines of the paragraph.

*Your Name*
*Date*

*The Weather*

　　*There are four seasons in Boston. The names of the seasons are winter, spring, summer, and autumn. In the winter it is often very cold and windy, and in the summer it is sometimes very hot and humid. The weather in the spring and autumn, however, is usually very pleasant. For many people, these are the two best seasons of the year because they are the only times the climate is comfortable. There is one thing certain about Boston weather. It never stays the same. It changes every few hours.*

It sometimes helps to think of a paragraph as a sandwich. The top and bottom layers (the first and last sentences) are general statements about the topic, and the filling (the middle sentences) statements of facts and examples. The top and bottom layers tie the paragraph together.

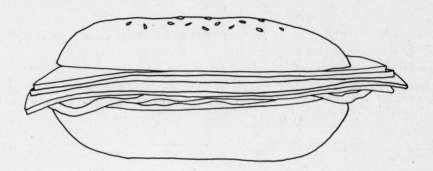

## WRITING MECHANICS

1. Put a title at the top in the center of the page.
2. Indent each paragraph.
3. Capitalize the first word of every sentence.
4. Put a period, question mark, or exclamation point at the end of every sentence.
5. Write on the lines.

# Parallel Paragraphs

Read this description of Michael Brown.

Michael Brown is a student at Stanford University. He is 5 feet 6 inches tall, and he weighs 160 pounds. He has straight black hair and dark eyes. He is studying economics because he hopes to become an economist.

---

**A.** Now write a similar description of (1) Robert Jones, (2) Mary Carlson, (3) Tom O'Neill, (4) Elizabeth Day, and (5) yourself. Use the pronoun *I* in (5).

1. Robert Jones — the University of Virginia — 6 feet — 180 pounds — short brown hair — hazel eyes — medicine — doctor

   Robert Jones is a studen at University of Virginia. He is 6 feet, and he weights 180 pounds. He has short brown hair and hazel eyes. He is studing medicine because he hopes to become a doctor.

2. Mary Carlson — Colorado State University — 5 feet 6 inches — 120 pounds — long blonde hair — blue eyes — medicine — doctor

   Mary Carlson is a student at Colorado State University. She is 5 feet 6 inches tall, and she weights 120 pounds. She has long blond hair and blue eyes. She is studing medicine because she hopes to become a doctr.

3. Tom O'Neill — the University of Wisconsin — 5 feet 10 inches — 175 pounds — curly red hair — light blue eyes — law — lawyer

   Tom O'Neill is a student the University of Wiscosin. He is 5 feet 10 inches tall, and he weights 175 pounds. He has curly red hair and light blue eyes. He is studing law he hopes to become a lawyer.

4. Elizabeth Day — Radcliffe College — ▮▮▮▮▮▮▮▮ ounds
   — dark brown hair — green eyes — chemistry — chemist

   *Elizabeth Day she is a student at the College. She is feets 6 inches tall. She has dark brown hair and green eyes. She is studing chemistry because she hopes to become a chemist.*

5. *Christopher Noreega is a student at Comille f. Rouge. He is 4 feet 5 inches tall and He has light brown hair and brown eyes. He is studing electrical engineerings because he hopes to become an electrical engerears.*

   Weights 86 pounds .

**B.** Write a sentence following the examples for each of the following fields of study and professions.

*She is studying medicine because she hopes to become a doctor.*
*or*
*He is studying medicine because he hopes to become a doctor.*

| Field of Study | Profession |
|---|---|
| medicine | doctor |
| engineering | engineer |
| education | teacher |
| law | lawyer |
| business administration | businessman/businesswoman |
| computer programming | computer programmer |
| fashion design | fashion designer |
| art | artist |
| physics | physicist |
| psychology | psychologist |

# Parallel Paragraphs

Read the paragraph about José Muñoz.

José Muñoz was born in Mexico, so his native language is Spanish. He has three brothers and no sisters. His favorite hobby is collecting postcards, and his favorite sport is baseball. He enjoys listening to Latin music. On weekends he likes to go to the movies.

---

**A.** Write a similar paragraph about (1) Silvia Pizano, (2) Mariko Yamada, and (3) Fahad Al-Saleh using the chart on the next page. Be sure to change the pronoun to *she* for females.

1. *Isabel Acevedo was born in Puerto Rico, so her native language is Spanish. She has three sisters no brothers. Her favorite hobby is go shopping and her favorite sport is baseball. She enjoys to watch TV. On weekends she likes to go side seen.*

2. *Conchita Acevedo was born in Puerto Rico, so her native language is Spanish. She has three sisters and no brothers. Her favorite hobby is go out to eat at the restaurant, and his favorite sport is boxing. She enjoys go out to have some drinks. On weekends she likes to go out for dinner.*

3. *Maria Acevedo was born in Puerto Rico, so her native language is Spanish. She has three sisters and no brothers. Her favorite hobby is go shopping and her favorite is sport swimming. She enjoys to do gets together at her home. On the weekends she likes to go out and eats at the restaurant.*

**B.** Pair off with another student in your class and ask him (or her) the following questions. Fill in the answers on the chart (4), and let your teacher check the answers.

1. Where were you born?
2. What is your native language?

| Name | José Muñoz (M) | (1) Silvia Pizano (F) | (2) Mariko Yamada (F) | (3) Fahad Al-Saleh (M) | (4) Classmate | (5) Yourself |
|---|---|---|---|---|---|---|
| Country | Mexico | Italy | Japan | Saudi Arabia | | |
| Language | Spanish | Italian | Japanese | Arabic | | |
| Brothers | three | two | none (0) | four | | |
| Sisters | none (0) | two | none (0) | three | | |
| Hobby | collecting post cards | painting with oils | photog-raphy | collecting stamps | | |
| Sport | baseball | swimming | skiing | soccer | | |
| Music | Latin music | jazz | classical music | disco | | |
| Weekends | go to movies | watch TV | go to concerts | visit friends | | |

(M) = male
(F) = female

3. How many brothers do you have?
4. How many sisters do you have?
5. What is your favorite hobby?
6. What is your favorite sport?
7. What kind of music do you enjoy listening to?
8. What do you like to do on weekends?
Now write a similar paragraph about your classmate.

*Paragraph about Classmate*

_____
_____
_____
_____
_____
_____

**C.** First fill in the chart (5) with the information about yourself, and then write a similar paragraph about yourself. Use the pronoun *I*.

*Paragraph about Yourself*

_____

_____

_____

_____

_____

**D.** Write a sentence following the example for each of the countries and native languages.

*He      was born in Colombia, so his native language is Spanish.*
*She                            her*

| *Country* | *Native language* |
|-----------|-------------------|
| Colombia | Spanish |
| Brazil | Portuguese |
| France | French |
| England | English |
| Saudi Arabia | Arabic |
| Germany | German |
| Italy | Italian |
| Japan | Japanese |
| Korea | Korean |
| Taiwan | Chinese |

_____

_____

_____

_____

_____

_____

_____

_____

_____

# Model Composition / The Weather

There are four seasons in Boston. The names of the seasons are winter, spring, summer, and autumn. In the winter it is often very cold and windy, and in the summer it is sometimes very hot and humid. The weather in the spring and autumn, however, is usually very pleasant. For many people, these are the two best seasons of the year because they are the only times the climate is comfortable. There is one thing certain about Boston weather. It never stays the same. It changes every few hours.

## Quotations

Everybody talks about the weather, but nobody does anything about it.
CHARLES DUDLEY WARNER

In New England in the spring, I have counted one hundred and thirty-six different kinds of weather in twenty-four hours.
MARK TWAIN

## COMPOSITION EXERCISES

### Comprehension Questions on the Model Composition

A. Working with a partner, answer in complete sentences. One student asks the question and the other student answers. (Alternate.)
1. How many seasons are there in Boston?
2. What are the names of the seasons?
3. How is the weather in the winter?
4. How is the weather in the summer?
5. How is the weather in the spring and autumn?
6. What are the two best seasons of the year for many people?
7. Is there anything certain about the weather in Boston?
8. What is certain about Boston weather?

### Common Expressions

1. He is a fair-weather friend.
2. A sunshiny shower
   Won't last half an hour.
   Rain before seven,
   Fair by eleven.

The South wind brings wet weather,
The North wind wet and cold together;
The West wind always brings us rain,
The East wind blows it back again.

March winds and April showers
Bring forth May flowers.

Red sky at night is the sailor's delight.
Red sky at morning, sailors, take warning.

*Unknown, Old Nursery Rhyme*

**B.  Vocabulary of Weather:**  Working with a partner, read the following dialogue. (Alternate questions and answers.)

*Adjective*

It is  fair.
    sunny.
    mild.
    warm.
    cool.
    hot.
    cold.
    windy.
    rainy.
    wet.
    humid.
    dry.

Student A: How is the weather today?
Student B: It is fair.
Student B: How is the weather today?
Student A: It is sunny.
            etc.

## STRUCTURE

### Adverbs of Frequency

Adverbs of frequency tell you how often something happens. Adverbs of frequency usually go before the main verb in a sentence, except for the verb *to be*. They go after the verb *to be*.

*Adverb of Frequency + Verb*

It  always      rains in the summer.

{ generally
 usually
 often
 frequently
{ sometimes
 occasionally
{ seldom
 rarely
 hardly ever
never

*to be + Adverb of Frequency*

It  is    always sunny.

{ generally
 usually
 often
 frequently
{ sometimes
 occasionally
{ seldom
 rarely
 hardly ever
never

**There is — There are**

In English, the usual word order for a statement sentence is *subject + verb*. The subject and verb must agree.

*Subject    +    Verb*

The child    is    happy.

The people    are    poor.

An exception to this rule of word order is the use of *there is* and *there are* at the beginning of a sentence followed by a noun and a place.

*Verb + Subject + Place*

There    is    a book    on the shelf.

There    are    children    in the park.

In these sentences the subject follows the verb and must agree with the verb. The word *there* has no meaning in these sentences. It is used to introduce the verb. It is called an *expletive*.

C.   Fill in the words *there is* or *there are* in the following sentences.
     *There are* books on the shelf.
     *There is*   a child in the park.

1. _____ two students from China in the class.

2. _____ one student from Korea here.

3. _____ some papers on the desk.

4. _____ a woman in the office.

5. _____ trees in the park.

6. _____ a bed in the bedroom.

7. _____ many people in the street.

8. _____ a cat in the house.

9. _____ coats in the closet.

10. _____ many cars on the road.

## DICTATION / DICTO-COMP

San Francisco is a naturally air-conditioned city. There is fresh air all year round. The summers are cool and the winters are mild. The sun shines most of the time, but it sometimes rains between November and March. It is often foggy in the morning from May to August, but it clears up in the afternoon. The evenings are cool and comfortable. Flowers bloom throughout the year. The wonderful climate is one reason why San Francisco is the tourist's favorite city.

## ACTIVITIES

**D.**  Prepare an *oral composition* about the weather in your city. Follow the sentence patterns in the model composition, and answer the following questions about your city.

*Oral Composition: The Weather in* _____
1. How many seasons are there in your city?
2. What are the names of the seasons?
3. How is the weather in the winter?
   in the spring?
   in the summer?
   in the autumn?
4. What is the best season of the year? Why?
5. Is there anything certain about the weather in your city?

## COMPOSITION WRITING

**E.**  Write a paragraph about "The Weather in My City" following the model composition and answering the above questions. Be sure to use correct paragraph form. Indent the first sentence.

*The Weather in* _____

# Model Composition / The Classroom

The English classroom is on the tenth floor of the Smith Building. It is a large room about twenty-five feet long and eighteen feet wide. The walls are light green and tan, and the ceiling is white. There are four windows on one side of the room. Under the windows, there are two radiators for heating the room in the wintertime. On the opposite wall, near one end, there is a brown door, and next to it there is a thermostat. There is a large blackboard on the front wall of the room with chalk and erasers on the ledge. The teacher's desk is in front of this blackboard. In the back of the room, there is a row of hooks on the wall for the students' coats and jackets. There are about twenty light-colored chairs in the room for the students. Each chair has a flat right arm. This arm is the student's desk. On the whole, it is a pleasant and comfortable room.

---

**Quotation**

Small rooms discipline the mind; large ones distract it.
LEONARDO DA VINCI

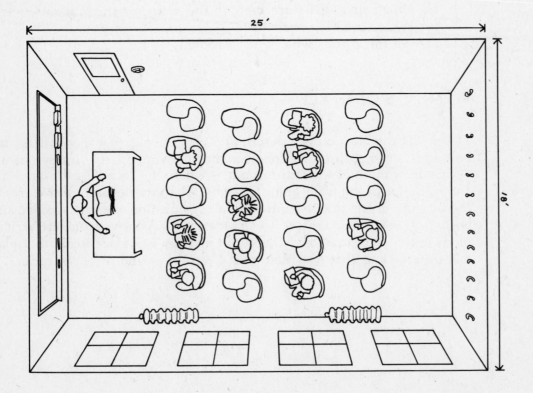

11

## COMPOSITION EXERCISES

### Common Expressions

*Expressions of Place*
on the tenth floor
on one side
under the windows
on the opposite wall
near one end
next to it
on the front wall
on the ledge
in front of the blackboard
in the back of the room
in the room

*Idioms*
on the whole

### Comprehension Questions on the Model Composition

A.
1. Where is the English classroom?
2. How large is it?
3. What color are the walls? What color is the ceiling?
4. What is under the windows?
5. What is on the opposite wall?
6. What is on the front wall of the room?
7. Where is the teacher's desk?
8. What is in the back of the room?
9. How many chairs are there in the room for the students?
10. What does each chair have?
11. On the whole, what kind of room is it?

## ELEMENTS OF STYLE

The model composition is a description of a room in *spatial order* organization. In this composition we followed the following order: First we started with a description of the entire room — where it is located, how large it is, and the color of the walls and the ceiling. Then we began to move around the room from one side to another. The organization of a spatial order composition is very important. It doesn't matter if you move from left to right, or from top to bottom, but you cannot go from one place to another place and then back to the first. You must keep some kind of organization.

## STRUCTURE

### More Expressions of Place

| | | | |
|---|---|---|---|
| at the top | across the street | in the corner of | |
| at the bottom | opposite the windows | on the right side of | |
| to the right/left | behind the chair | on the left side of | } the room |
| in the center | in a room | in the middle of | |
| over the bed | on a wall | | |
| above the bed | around the table | | |
| below the ceiling | | | |

to the right of  } the table            by    } the window
to the left of                          near

**B.** Working with a partner, fill in the blanks with the correct prepositions.

My room is _____ the first floor _____ a building _____ _____ Philadelphia, Pennsylvania. It is a large room about twenty-three feet long and eighteen feet wide. The walls are light blue and the ceiling is white. _____ one side of the room there are three windows. _____ the opposite wall, _____ the middle, there is a brown door and _____ to it, there is a light switch. There is a large bed _____ one corner _____ the room. _____ the bed there is a painting of a landscape. _____ to the bed, there is a night table. _____ the night table, there is a lamp. _____ the other side _____ the night table, there is a closet. \_\_\_\_\_ _____ the other side _____ the room there is a sofa. _____ the left side _____ the sofa, there is a television set. _____ the right side _____ the sofa, there is a little end table and _____ this table there is a radio. _____ the center of the room _____ the floor, there is a blue Oriental carpet. There is a nice table with four chairs _____ it on this carpet. A white tablecloth and a bowl of flowers are _____ the table. On the whole, it is a cheerful and comfortable room.

## ACTIVITIES

**C.** **Describing a room you have designed:** Working in a group, design a room and describe it. Have one person draw the diagram as the group decides where to put the furnishings. Try to give a color to each object.

When the diagram is finished, write a group composition. Everyone writes the composition individually, but you all must agree on the organization and on each sentence structure (follow outline F). Everyone in the group will have the same composition. When everyone in the group has finished writing the composition, attach the diagram of the room the group has designed to the compositions. Everyone in the group should sign the diagram.

**D. Questions About Your Own Classroom** (Oral or Written): The answers to these questions will be the composition about your own classroom.

1. Where is your classroom? (floor and building)
2. How large is it?
3. What color are the walls and what color is the ceiling?
4. What is on one wall?
5. What is under the windows?
6. What is on the opposite wall?
7. What else is on the wall?
8. What is on the front wall of the room?
9. What is in front of this blackboard?
10. What is in the back of the room?
11. What else is there in the room?
12. Where do the students sit?
13. Is the room usually light and airy?
14. Is it pleasant and comfortable?

**E.** Now write a paragraph describing your classroom, following the model composition and answering the above questions.

## DICTATION / DICTO-COMP

My room is on the fourth floor of a building at 119 Park Place. It is a large room about twenty feet long and sixteen feet wide. The walls are white, and the ceiling is too. On one wall there are two windows. On the opposite wall, there is a bed and a closet. Between the bed and the closet there is a white door leading into the bathroom. There is a large desk against the front wall of the room with my books, my notebook, my dictionary, my pens, my pencils, and my lamp on it. My chair is in front of the desk. In the back of the room there is a chest of drawers and a refrigerator. There is also a small table and a yellow armchair in the room and an orange rug on the floor. On the whole, it is a pleasant and comfortable room.

## COMPOSITION WRITING

**F.** Write a composition about one room where you live, using the outline and following the model composition. Try to follow the model as much as possible. Be sure to use expressions of place and to vary the placement of them in your sentences.

*Description of a Room*
A. General Description (entire room)
    1. Where is your room? (location)
    2. How large is it? (size)
    3. What color are the walls and the ceiling? (color)
B. Details (organization of the room by space)
    1. What is on one wall?
    2. What is on the opposite wall?
    3. What is on the other walls?
    4. Where is the door?
    5. Where is the furniture?
    6. What else is in the room?
C. Concluding Sentence (entire room)
    1. Is it a pleasant and comfortable room? (atmosphere)

# Model Composition / A Letter to a Friend

July 18, 19 ____

Dear Maria,

It is three o'clock in the afternoon now, and I am sitting in the library and writing you this letter. It is a very pleasant, warm summer day, and I am looking out the window at Jefferson Park. There are lots of people in the park today. There are many parents and children in the playground. The children are playing games and chasing each other. The parents are standing or sitting in groups and talking to each other. Some mothers and fathers are running after their children. There are many elderly people in the park this afternoon, too. Some are reading newspapers, and some are just resting on the benches. There are also a lot of college students in the park today. Some of the young men and women are walking in the park and holding hands. (This isn't usual in our country, but this custom is quite common here.) There are lots of good-looking men in the park today also, and I am very busy people-watching. This is one of my favorite pastimes. It is more interesting than doing homework. However, I must say "Good-by" and get back to my work.

Fondly,
Carla

## Quotation

If you want to discover your true opinion of anybody, observe the impression made on you by the first sight of a letter from him.

SCHOPENHAUER

## COMPOSITION EXERCISES

### Common Expressions

to look out the window
to talk to someone
to run after someone
to hold hands
to get back

**Comprehension Questions on the Model Composition**

A. Make believe you are the writer of the model composition, and answer in complete sentences.
1. What time is it?
2. Where are you sitting?
3. What kind of day is it?
4. Are there any people in the park today?
5. Are there lots of parents and children in the playground?
6. What are the children doing?
7. What are the parents doing?
8. Are there a lot of elderly people in the park today?
9. What are they doing?
10. Are there many college students in the park today?
11. What are some of the young men and women doing?
12. Are there many good-looking men in the park today?
13. What are you doing?

## STRUCTURE

**Use of** *many/much/a lot of/lots of*

many
a lot of  } + countable nouns (plural)
lots of

Are there *many* students in the class?
Are there *a lot of* students in the class?
Are there *lots of* students in the class?

much
a lot of  } + uncountable nouns (singular)
lots of

Is there *much* noise in the room?
Is there *a lot of* noise in the room?
Is there *lots of* noise in the room?

Note: *Much* is not usually used in affirmative statements. *A lot of* and *lots of* are not usually used in negative statements.

*There is a lot of* noise in the street.
*There isn't much* noise in this room.

B. Rewrite the following sentences using (a) *a lot of* and (b) *lots of.*
There are *many* children in the park today.
There are *a lot of* children in the park today.
There are *lots of* children in the park today.
1. Is there *much* furniture in the room?

_____

_____

2. Are there *many* people in the street?

_____

_____

3. There are *many* students in this class.

_____

_____

4. Do you have *much* money?

_____

_____

5. He has *many* friends.

_____

_____

**C.** Working with a partner, fill in the blanks with the correct form of the verb in parentheses in the following paragraph.

April 2, 19 _____

Dear Peter,

It _____ (be) eleven o'clock in the morning, and I _____ _____ (sit) in the classroom and _____ (write) you this letter. It _____ (be) a warm day outside, but inside my classmates _____ (be) very busy. There _____ (be) fifteen foreign students in the class, and all of them _____ (try) to learn English. There _____ (be) two students from Greece. One _____ (read), while the other _____ (talk) to a classmate. There _____ (be) three students from the Far East. One _____ (be) from Korea, another _____ (be) from Taiwan, and the third _____ (be) from Malaysia. The student from Korea _____ (look) at the blackboard, while the other two _____ (write) in their notebooks. There _____ (be) seven Spanish-speaking students in the class. Most of them _____ (be) from Latin America, but one _____ (be) from Spain. The student from Spain _____ (look up) a word in his dictionary, while the Latin American students _____ (listen to) the teacher. A woman from Poland and a man from Haiti _____ (be) also in this class. The Polish student _____ (sit) in the front row and _____ (think about) her country, while the

Haitian student _____ (sit) in the back row and _____

_____ (click) his pen. The teacher _____

(stand) in front of the room. I _____ (be) the only student in the

class from France.

It _____ (be) almost time for lunch, so I must stop writing now

and get back to my English lessons.

Your friend,
Nicole


## ACTIVITIES

**D.** Write a composition in the form of a letter to a friend, following the model composition and describing the scene and activities. Write it from your classroom. (Follow model and Exercise C.)

1. Tell your friend what time it is and where you are sitting.
2. Tell your friend what kind of day it is.
3. Tell your friend who is in the classroom.
4. Tell your friend what they are doing.


## DICTATION / DICTO-COMP

February 12, 19____

Dear Jimmy,

It is one o'clock in the afternoon, and I am sitting in the coffee house and writing you this letter. It is a cold, snowy day outside, but the coffee house is below street level, so it is windowless. There are many people in the coffee house today. Three fellows are sitting at a table next to me. They are having lunch and talking about the political situation. Two young men with beards are sitting in a corner of the room and playing chess. At another table, there are four people who look like students. I think they are doing their home-work. There is a food counter near the door of the coffee house. Three young women are standing in front of the counter. Two are buying sand-wiches, and the third is paying for her lunch. The coffee house is very crowded and noisy today. It is very interesting to sit and people-watch, but I must say "Good-by" now and get back to my work.

Sincerely yours,
Bill

# COMPOSITION WRITING

**E.** Write a letter to a friend from the lobby of a hotel, or the airport, or the school cafeteria, or a café in your country, etc. (Follow the model, and use letter form.)

*A Letter to a Friend*

A. Opening (generalization)
   1. Time of day (What time is it?)
   2. Setting (Where are you sitting?)
   3. Weather (What kind of day is it?)
B. Specific Description of Scene
   1. Groups of people (Who is there?)
   2. Activities (What are they doing?)
C. Closing (generalization)

# Model Composition / The United States

The United States is a very large country. From the East Coast to the West Coast it is about 3000 miles wide. The Atlantic Ocean is on the East Coast, and the Pacific Ocean is on the West Coast. Canada is the country to the north of the United States, and Mexico is the country to the south. The Rio Grande River is the boundary between Mexico and the United States. The major mountain ranges are the Appalachian Mountains in the East and the Rocky Mountains in the West. There are many rivers in the United States. The most important ones are the Mississippi and the Missouri Rivers in the central part of the country, and the Colorado and Columbia Rivers in the West. The country is a composite of different geographic formations — high mountains and deep canyons, great river systems and landlocked lakes, rolling plains, forests and rocky coasts, sandy beaches, and even deserts. There are fifty states in the Union today. The two newest states, Hawaii and Alaska, are geographically separated from the other forty-eight states.

The United States is a heterogeneous country. The American people are of almost every race, every creed, and every nationality. This is because of the great immigration from abroad throughout American history. The population is now over 232 million people*, including 1.3 million Native Americans. English is the common language.

*1983 figure

---

**Directional Points**

North
South
East
West

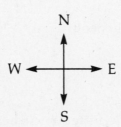

**Quotations**

It is easier to understand a nation by listening to its music than by learning its language.

ANONYMOUS

What makes a nation great is not primarily its great men, but the stature of its innumerable mediocre ones.

ORTEGA Y GASSET

## COMPOSITION EXERCISES

### Comprehension Questions on the Model Composition

**A.**
1. How large is the United States?
2. Where is the Atlantic Ocean? Where is the Pacific Ocean?
3. What country is to the north? What country is to the south?
4. What river is the boundary between the United States and Mexico?
5. What are the major mountain ranges?
6. What are the most important rivers in the United States?
7. How many states are there in the United States now?
8. What are the two newest states?
9. How large is the population of the United States today?
10. What is the common language?

### Vocabulary and Common Expressions

mountain ranges
a composite
geographic formations
canyons
river systems
landlocked
rolling plains
forests
rocky coasts
sandy beaches
deserts
to be geographically apart
creed
immigration vs. emigration
heterogeneous vs. homogeneous

## STRUCTURE

### Rules for the Use of the Definite Article Before Geographical Place Names

1. Use the definite article with the names of all bodies of water except individual lakes.

   | | |
   |---|---|
   | the Pacific Ocean | the Red Sea |
   | the Atlantic Ocean | the Black Sea |
   | the Mississippi River | the English Channel |
   | the Suez Canal | the Persian Gulf |

2. Use the definite article before the names of deserts and forests.

   | | |
   |---|---|
   | the Black Forest | the Sahara Desert |

3. Use the definite article before all plural names.

   | | |
   |---|---|
   | the British Isles | the Great Lakes |
   | the Philippines | the Rocky Mountains |
   | the Netherlands | the Andes Mountains |

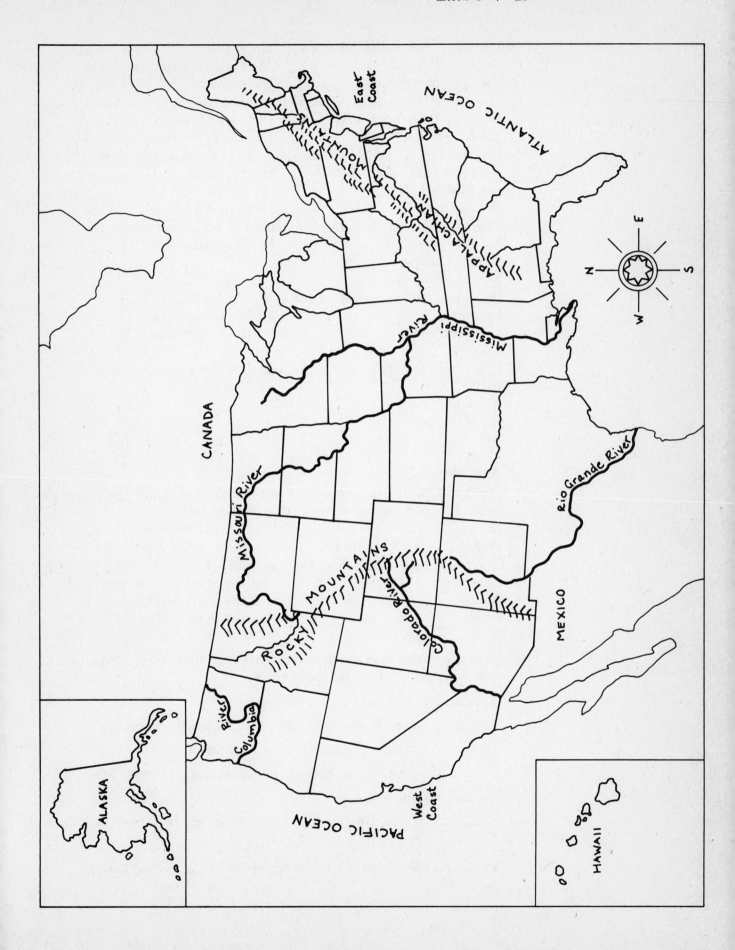

4. Use the definite article before all names that end in an *of* phrase.
the Bay of Biscay                the Peoples' Republic of China
the Gulf of Mexico               the University of New Mexico

5. Use the definite article before all names that designate a political union.
the British *Commonwealth*       the *United* States
the Dominican *Republic*         the *Union* of Soviet Socialist Republics

6. Use the definite article before the names of geographic areas.
the Near East                    the Far West
the Middle East                  the Orient
the Far East                     the Occident

7. Don't use the article before the names of individual mountains.
Mont Blanc                       *but* The Matterhorn
Mount Everest
Mount Whitney

8. Don't use the article before the names of individual lakes.
Lake Erie                        *but* the Great Lakes
Lake Lucerne                         the Finger Lakes
Lake Placid

9. Don't use the article before the names of cities or continents.
Paris                            *but* The Hague
Istanbul
Caracas
Asia
Europe
Australia

10. Don't use the article before the name of a country where the country's name does not include a word for a political union.
Peru            Korea            Mexico
France          India            Canada

11. Don't use the article before the names of states.
New Jersey                       *but* the State of New Jersey
Illinois                             the State of Illinois
California                           the State of Florida
Ohio

**B.**  Fill in the blanks with the definite article *the*, if necessary. If no article is necessary, put an X in the blank space.

1. _____ France is in _____ Europe.

2. _____ Andes Mountains are in _____ South America.

3. _____ Tokyo is the capital of _____ Japan.

4. _____ St. Lawrence River is between _____ United States and _____ Canada.

5. _____ Sahara Desert in _____ Africa extends from _____ Atlantic Ocean to _____ Nile River.

6. _____ Lake Superior is the largest of _____ Great Lakes.

7. _____ Mount Everest in _____ Nepal is the highest mountain in the world.

8. _____ Black Forest is in _____ Germany.

9. _____ Bay of Biscay is between _____ Spain and _____ France.

10. Caracas is the capital of _____ Venezuela.

**C.** Fill in the blanks with the definite article *the*, if necessary. If no article is necessary, put an X in the blank space.

_____ Alaska, the forty-ninth state, entered the Union in 1959. The capital of _____ Alaska is _____ Juneau. _____ Alaska is bounded on the north by _____ Arctic Ocean, on the east by _____ Canada, on the south by _____ Pacific Ocean, and on the west by _____ Bering Sea. The major rivers are _____ Yukon, _____ Tanana, and _____ Kuskokwim. The highest mountain in _____ North America, _____ Mount McKinley, is in _____ Alaska. _____ Alaska is the largest state in the Union.

## Rules of Capitalization

1. Capitalize the first word in every sentence.
   The pen is yellow.

2. Capitalize all proper names (and nouns used as proper names).
   a. Names of people, nationalities, and races.

   | | | |
   |---|---|---|
   | Jack Kennedy | English | Negro |
   | Mary | South American | Oriental |
   | | Hungarian | |
   | | Turkish | |

   b. Specific geographical locations.

   | | | |
   |---|---|---|
   | London | Peru | the Mississippi River |
   | Mount Everest | Fifth Avenue | |

   c. Names of languages.

   Spanish    Turkish    French    Chinese

   d. Points on the compass when they indicate a section of the country.
   the East (but eastern United States).
   the West

   e. Days of the week, months, and holidays.

   | | | |
   |---|---|---|
   | Friday | June | Thanksgiving Day |
   | Saturday | July | Christmas |

   f. Names of religions, deities, and items of sacred significance.

   | | | |
   |---|---|---|
   | Buddhism | Jehova | the Blessed Virgin |
   | Judaism | Allah | |
   | Catholicism | | |

   g. A title preceding a proper noun.

   | | |
   |---|---|
   | Princess Caroline | Professor Miller |
   | Queen Elizabeth | President Lincoln |

## DICTATION / DICTO-COMP

The United States is sometimes called a salad bowl of nationalities. According to the 1980 census, more than 118 million people traced their ancestry back to one foreign country, while nearly 70 million listed more than one country as their ethnic homeland. The report stated that 26.34 percent of Americans listed England as their country of ethnic origin. Germany was second with 26.14 percent. The Irish were the third-largest ethnic group; the Afro-Americans were the fourth with 11.13 percent; and the French were the fifth with 6.85 percent. This is why many people say that if you scratch an American, you will find the world.

**Largest Ancestry Groups Reported Ranked in Descending Order***

| | |
|---|---|
| English | 49,598,035 |
| German | 49,224,146 |
| Irish | 40,165,702 |
| Afro-American | 20,964,729 |
| French | 12,892,246 |
| Italian | 12,183,692 |
| Scottish | 10,048,816 |
| Polish | 8,228,037 |
| Mexican | 7,692,619 |

*Reported by 100,000 or more Americans according to Census Bureau Report on Ancestry of Americans, 1980.

## ACTIVITIES

**D.** Prepare an *Oral Composition*, for presentation to the class, about your country by answering the following questions.

1. Where is your native country located?
2. How large is it?
3. What are the boundaries? (What lies to the east, the west, the north, the south?)
4. What are the major mountain ranges, if any?
5. What are the most important rivers, if any?
6. What is the general topography of the country?
7. What races(s) and creed(s) are the people in your country?
8. How large is the population?
9. What is the common language?

# COMPOSITION WRITING

**E.** Write a two-paragraph composition following the model and the outline below.

*My Country*

I. Physical Characteristics (First Paragraph)
  A. Size
      1. Large or small
      2. Area in square miles
  B. Boundaries
      1. Natural: oceans, rivers, mountain ranges
      2. Political: national frontiers
  C. Principal Geographic Features
      1. Mountain ranges
      2. Rivers, lakes
      3. Deserts or jungles
  D. Subdivisions of the Country
      1. Number of divisions (states, districts, etc.)
      2. Geographically separated divisions (if any)

II. The People (Second Paragraph)
  A. Background
      1. Origin
      2. Diversity
  B. Population Size
  C. Common Language

# Model Composition / What Am I?

I usually go to work by limousine or taxi. I start work at different times, and I sometimes have to work nights, holidays, and weekends. Before I go to work, I put on my uniform. I usually take a small bag with me to work because on an overseas flight I have a twenty-four to thirty hour layover before I have a return flight. Then I am off for a few days. My job takes me all over the world.

My work is usually pleasant and sometimes exciting. I meet all kinds of people and talk to everyone. I try to make everyone comfortable, and I give special attention to elderly passengers and to children traveling alone. I show people what to do in case of an emergency. I know how to give first aid and what to do in case of a highjacking, bomb threat, or forced landing. During mealtimes, I serve the passengers food, and I always ask, "Coffee or tea?" Most passengers are polite, but sometimes a passenger is rude. I never start and finish my work in the same place.

*Airline flight attendant*

## Quotations

To youth I have but three words of counsel — work, work, work.

BISMARCK

Many hands make light work.

WILLIAM PATTEN

It is work which gives flavor to life.

AMIEL

There is no substitute for hard work.

THOMAS ALVA EDISON

## COMPOSITION EXERCISES

### Comprehension Questions on the Model Composition

A. 1. How does he usually go to work?
2. What time does he start to work?
3. When does he sometimes have to work?
4. What does he do before he goes to work?
5. What does he usually take with him?
6. How long is his layover?
7. Where does his job take him?
8. What kind of people does he meet?
9. What does he try to do?

10. To whom does he give special attention?
11. What does he know how to do?
12. What does he do during mealtimes?
13. Are passengers polite or rude?
14. Does he start and finish his work in the same place?

**Vocabulary and Common Expressions**

| | | | |
|---|---|---|---|
| hijacking | | limousine | to put on |
| bomb threat | | car | to have a layover |
| forced landing | by | train | to be off |
| polite/rude | | bus | to give first aid |
| | | taxi | |

**Questions on Vocabulary and Common Expressions**

B.
1. How do you go to work (school)?
2. What do you put on in the wintertime?
3. Are people usually off work on Saturdays in your country?
4. Do you know how to give first aid?
5. Where does a flight from the U.S. to Japan sometimes have a layover?
6. Are most people in this country polite or rude?

## STRUCTURE

C. Fill in the blanks with the correct form of the verb in parentheses. Use the present simple tense.

Ms. X _____ (get up) at 7:00 A.M. every morning. It _____ (take) her about half an hour to get ready. She _____ (leave) home at 7:30. She _____ (drive) to work. She _____ (arrive) at her office at about 8:00 A.M. and _____ (start) to work. She usually _____ (eat) lunch at 1:00 P.M., and she sometimes _____ (take) a fifteen-minute break in the afternoon. She usually _____ (leave) for home at 5:00 P.M.

Ms. X _____ (enjoy) her job very much. She _____ (help) and _____ (advise) people. She _____ (try) to be helpful to everyone. She always _____ (stay—*negative*) in her office because she often _____ (have to) be in court to defend somebody. She

_____ (have) a good reputation, and people _____

_____ (respect) her. Her purpose in life _____ (be) to

serve justice and to defend everyone's rights. Ms. X is a lawyer.

## DICTATION / DICTO-COMP

I usually go to work by subway. I get to work by 8:00 A.M. Before I start my job, I put on my uniform and look at myself in the mirror to make sure that I look neat. At 8:30 in the morning, I go on duty. I usually eat lunch from twelve to one and generally take a fifteen-minute break in the morning and in the afternoon. At 4:30 in the afternoon, I go off duty.

I enjoy my job very much. I meet all kinds of people and talk to everyone. Many people ask me questions, and I give them the necessary information. I try to be very helpful. I always call out floors very clearly. I never stay in one place long. On the contrary, I am constantly on the move. Most men take off their hats in my car. Sometimes I tell passengers to put out their cigarettes. Some people smile at me, and others ignore me. My life is a series of "ups" and "downs."

*Elevator operator*

## COMPOSITION WRITING

**D.** Write a composition in the third person singular about someone's job. Use Ms. X or Mr. Y as the subject. Try to follow the model for organization, and use the following questions as a guide.

What is she?  
        he? } (Ms. X or Mr. Y)

I. First Paragraph
 1. How does she(he) get to work?
 2. What time does she(he) start to work?
 3. What does she(he) do before she(he) starts her(his) job?
 4. What time does she(he) finish work?

II. Second Paragraph
 1. Does she(he) enjoy her(his) job?
 2. Whom does she(he) meet?
 3. What does she(he) do on her(his) job?
 4. Does she(he) stay in one place or does she(he) move around?
 5. Closing sentence: Final sentence about Ms. X or Mr. Y and the job.

Up to here —

— Writing —

# Model Composition / A Comparison of Two Cities (Shanghai and New York)

Shanghai is different from New York in many ways, but there are many things that are similar.

Shanghai is one of the most populated cities in Asia, and New York is one of the most populated cities in North America. The weather in the summer is very hot in Shanghai, and it is the same in New York. Shanghai is a port and an industrial city, and New York is too. Shanghai has a problem with pollution, and New York has a similar problem. They both have serious traffic problems.

The traffic problem in Shanghai is caused by too many bicycles. The traffic problem in New York, on the other hand, is caused by too many automobiles. The population of Shanghai is homogeneous, but the population of New York is heterogeneous. Most of the people in Shanghai live in apartments in low buildings, while most of the people in New York live in apartments in high buildings. People eat with chopsticks in Shanghai, but they eat with knives and forks in New York. While there are some differences, the major problems of big cities are almost the same everywhere in the world.

## Quotations

Fields and trees teach me nothing, but the people in a city do.
SOCRATES (explaining why he rarely left the city)

The people are the city.
SHAKESPEARE

## COMPOSITION EXERCISES

### Common Expressions

*Vocabulary of Similarities*
the same as
to be the same
to be similar (to)
both

*Vocabulary of Differences*
to be different from
while
on the other hand
but

### Comprehension Questions on Model Composition

A.  1. Is Shanghai different from New York in any way?
2. Are there any things that are similar?
3. Compare the population of the two cities.
4. Compare the weather in Shanghai with the weather in New York.
5. Name one problem of Shanghai that is similar to a problem in New York.

6. What other problems do they both have?
7. What is the traffic problem in Shanghai caused by?
8. What is the traffic problem in New York caused by?
9. What is the difference between the population of Shanghai and the population of New York?
10. Compare the way the people in Shanghai and New York live.
11. Compare the way the people in Shanghai and New York eat.
12. Are the problems of all big cities very different?

## ELEMENTS OF STYLE

### Comparison and Contrast

A *comparison* tells you what things are the same about two things.
A *contrast* tells you what things are different about two things.

The composition makes use of sentences with parallel elements to show differences and similarities. Balanced sentences (where parallel constructions are equal in length) are fairly common for comparisons and contrasts.

The population of Shanghai is homogeneous, but the population of New York is heterogeneous.

Shanghai is one of the most populated cities in Asia, and New York is one of the most populated cities in North America.

There are many rich people in New York, but there are many poor people too. While the cost of entertainment is generally high, there are many free lectures, concerts, and exhibits.

## STRUCTURE

B.  Combine each of the following groups of sentences to make one balanced sentence with the indicated connectors.

Shanghai is in Asia.
New York is in North America.    (but)

*Shanghai is in Asia, but New York is in North America.*

1. The people in Shanghai use fans to keep cool.
   The people in New York use air-conditioning.   (while)

2. There are many high bridges in New York.
   There are many deep tunnels in New York.   (and)

3. There are many cathedrals in New York.   (while — start the
   There are many night clubs too.   sentence with *while*)

4. New York has many dirty streets.
   New York has many beautiful avenues.   (and)

5. The people in Shanghai speak Chinese.
   The people in New York speak English.   (but)

# DICTATION / DICTO-COMP

To most visitors, New York is both a fascinating and a frightening city. It is a city of great wealth and of great poverty. There are many rich people, but there are many poor people too. There are many luxury apartment buildings, and there are many slum tenements. There is a great deal of beauty and a great deal of ugliness. The parks and the shops are beautiful, but the dirty streets and the subway stations are ugly. There are many tall skyscrapers above ground and many winding subways under ground. Most things are expensive, but some things are free. The cost of entertainment is generally high, but there are usually many free lectures, concerts, and art exhibits. There is an "East Side" and a "West Side" and an "Uptown" and a "Downtown." There are people who work all day and people who work all night. The city is never asleep. New York seems unfriendly, but it really isn't.

## Vocabulary

*Opposites*
fascinating — frightening
wealth — poverty (noun)
rich — poor
luxury apartment buildings — slum tenements
beauty — ugliness (noun)
beautiful — ugly (adjective)
above ground — under ground
East Side — West Side
Uptown — Downtown
all day — all night

## Word Forms

| *Adjective* | *Noun** |
| --- | --- |
| wealthy | wealth |
| poor | poverty |
| beautiful | beauty |
| ugly | ugliness |

*All the nouns in this list are abstract nouns. Abstract nouns are usually uncountable and in the singular form.

Is there much $\begin{Bmatrix} \text{beauty} \\ \text{ugliness} \\ \text{wealth} \\ \text{poverty} \end{Bmatrix}$ in New York?

## ACTIVITIES

C. **Combining Sentences:** Working with a partner, combine each group of sentences to make one sentence. Use the connectors *and, but,* and *while* in sentences 1-6. The sentences will make a contrast paragraph. The first sentence in the paragraph will be:

*New York is a city of contrasts.*

1. There are many kind and helpful people.
   There are many dangerous people.
2. Many people are rich.
   Many people are poor.
3. There are many old people.
   There are many young people.
4. You can freeze in the winter.
   You can melt in the summer.
5. There are many dirty streets.
   There are many beautiful avenues.
6. There are symphony concerts.
   There are jazz concerts.
7. New York is a jungle.
   New York is a paradise. (Combine with the word *both*.)

## COMPOSITION WRITING

D. Write a composition of comparison and contrast about two cities following the model composition. First, fill in the outline with the things that you are going to compare and contrast. Use the same topic sentence with the names of the two cities you are going to write about. Be sure to use expressions of similarities and differences and parallel structures in your composition.

*Compa*

I. M _____ is different from _____ in many ways, bu_____ gs that are similar. (generalization)

II. Si_____
   A.
   B.
   C.
   D.

III. Difi_____
   A.
   B.
   C.
   D.
   E. Closing Sentence (generalization)

(Some things to compare: climate, people, industry, scenery, food and drink, political structure, family life, clothes, traffic, buildings, sports, transportation, etc.)

*Lesson* **7**

# Model Composition / Political Speech

Fellow Chicagoans! This is your mayor speaking. Chicago is facing a financial crisis. The city is heavily in debt, and we are going to have to increase taxes. We are going to need more money for low income housing. We are going to need more money for the city's schools. We are going to need more money for the transit system and for the police department. I plan to ask the state and the federal government to help us.

Chicago is a city divided racially now, and that cannot be. I hope to solve the problems of racial division. I am going to strive for unity. Chicago is going to be a united city. I intend to be the mayor of all Chicago. I want to reach out my hand in friendship and fellowship to everyone in the city. I need your help.

It is going to take the cooperation of every Chicagoan. Together, we are going to solve the city's problems. We are going to make Chicago "the city that works."

---

### Quotations

He serves his party best who serves his country best.
  RUTHERFORD B. HAYES (19th President of the United States)

You can't adopt politics as a profession and remain honest.

LOUIS McHENRY HOWE

## COMPOSITION EXERCISES

### Comprehension Questions on the Model Composition

A.  1. What kind of crisis is Chicago facing?
 2. Why is Chicago going to need more money?
 3. How does the mayor plan to raise the money?
 4. What kind of city is Chicago now?
 5. What is the mayor going to strive for?
 6. Whose cooperation is it going to take?
 7. What kind of city is the mayor going to make Chicago?

### Vocabulary and Common Expressions

to face a crisis
to be in debt
to ask someone to do something
to solve a problem

to strive for something
to abolish something
It is going to take . . .
to do one's part

39

### Questions on Vocabulary and Common Expressions

**B.**  1. Is your country facing a political crisis?
2. Is your government in debt? Are you in debt now?
3. What does the teacher often ask you to do?
4. What is it going to take to pass this course? (lots of work)
5. What are you striving to learn now? (the English language)
6. Will we ever be able to abolish hunger in the world?

## STRUCTURE

### Use of Infinitives after Certain Verbs

I *plan to ask* the state to help.   I *plan to take* a vacation next week.

I *want to reach out* my hand in   I *want to go* to the movies.
  friendship.

I *intend to be* the mayor of all Chicago.   I *intend to be* an engineer.

I *hope to solve* the problem.   I *hope to get* a better job.

**C.**  Answer the following questions.
1. What do you plan to do this weekend?
2. What do you hope to learn this semester?
3. What do you intend to do tonight?
4. What do you want to become in the future?

### Future Time Expressions

Notice the following constructions:

*going to* + verb — for planned or intended action
  I *am going to see* a movie tonight.

*will* + verb — promise, or statement of simple futurity
  I *will see* you tomorrow.

**D.**  Working with a partner, fill in the correct tense of the verb in parentheses. Try to use the *to be going* future form wherever possible.

Fellow students! This _____ (be) the president of your university speaking. The university _____ _____ (face) a financial crisis. The university _____ _____ (be) heavily in debt, and we _____ (need) more money to make this a better school in the years ahead. We _____ (need) more money for student dormitories. We _____ (need) more money for a gymnasium. We _____ (need) more money for research laboratories. We _____ (need) more money for faculty salaries.

I _____ (hope) to raise this money as painlessly as possible. I _____ (plan) to obtain money by various means. I _____ (ask) the state and the federal government to help. I _____ (ask) alumni and private individuals to do their part.

I _____ (intend — *negative*) to raise the tuition unless it _____ (be) absolutely necessary. I certainly _____ (hope) this necessity _____ (arise — *negative*).

It _____ (take) the cooperation of every student and every faculty and staff member. We _____ (solve) the university's problems. Together, we _____ (make) this university the best university in the country.

## The Conjunction *unless*

The conjunction *unless* means *if . . . not*.

> I don't intend to raise the tuition *if* it is*n't* absolutely necessary.
> I don't intend to raise the tuition *unless* it is absolutely necessary.
> *If* you do*n't* go, I won't go.
> *Unless* you go, I won't go.

**E.** Substitute the word *unless* for *if . . . not*.

1. I will go if I'm not too tired.

   _____

2. If they don't leave now, they will be late.

   _____

3. We can't call him if he doesn't give us his telephone number.

   _____

4. Mary won't write to you if you don't write to her first.

   _____

5. If you don't study, you won't pass the test.

   _____

## DICTATION / DICTO-COMP

The future is a world in which houses with brains will talk to the house next door. Men and women will "telecommunicate" to work in their living rooms. Families with problems will contact their electronic psychiatrist. Art will consist of computer-generated pictures. Kitchen computers will program food from freezer to microwave oven. They will supply a Mexican dinner complete with Mexican background music. Robots will cook and serve meals, and all walls will become video screens.

(From a speech Mr. Ray Mason of *Futurist Magazine* gave on July 6, 1983 in Las Vegas, Nevada.)

## COMPOSITION WRITING

**F.** Write a composition following the model composition and the outline below. Make believe you are one of the following: the president of a country, a school, a club, a university; the mayor of a city; the head of a business or professional group; or the teacher telling about the semester's work. (Complete the outline first.)

*Speech Outline*
  I. Reason for the Speech (generalization)
     A. Introduction
        1. Salutation
        2. Who is speaking?
     B. Problems Faced
        1. What are the problems?
           a.
           b.
        2. What are you going to need?
           a.
           b.
 II. Means of Solving the Problems
     A. How are you going to solve the problems?
        1.
        2.
     B. Conclusion (generalization)
        1. Whose cooperation is it going to take?
        2. What are the results going to be?

# Model Composition / Process Composition

**Model #1   How to Scramble Eggs**

Ingredients:   3 eggs
 ¼ teaspoon salt
 Dash pepper
 3 tablespoons milk or cream
 1 tablespoon butter

  Beat eggs slightly until yolks and whites are broken, but not too well mixed. Add salt, pepper, and milk. Now mix. Heat butter in skillet until melted and hot enough to sizzle when a drop of egg is added. Add eggs, reduce heat and cook slowly, stirring the eggs from the bottom as they become firm and browned slightly. Serve as soon as eggs are fairly firm (but not dry) throughout. Garnish with slices of crisp bacon. Serves two.

---

**Model #2   A Magic Trick: Linking Paper Clips**

  To perform a magic trick, linking paper clips together, you will need two paper clips and a paper money bill. First, fold a paper money bill in thirds as shown in the diagram. Then, place one clip around the first and second folds. Next, place the other clip around the second and third folds. Finally, pull the upper corners away from you in a quick motion. The paper clips will link together and drop to the table. Practice this at home until you get the knack.

## Model #3   Giving Directions (see map illustration)

To get to Macy's from here, turn to your right after leaving this building. Walk three blocks along Washington Square North until you come to Sixth Avenue. Turn right at the corner of Sixth Avenue, and walk one block north to Eighth Street. Don't cross the street. At the corner of Eighth Street and Sixth Avenue, you will see a newsstand and, near it, a sign marked "Bus Stop." Wait there until a #5 bus comes along. Get on the bus and tell the driver to let you off at 34th Street. When you get to 34th street, get off the bus. Cross the street to the side where there is a large building with a big clock over the door, and you will be at Macy's.

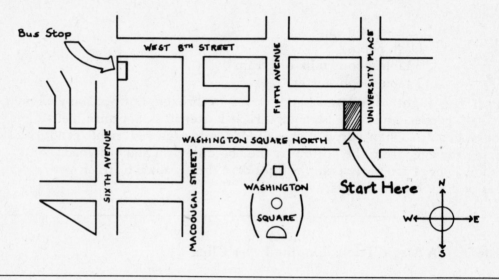

## Model #4   How to Use Chopsticks

Using chopsticks is not as difficult as it may seem. First, pick up the two chopsticks so that the squared ends are at the top. Make sure they are even by tapping them against a plate. Always keep the lower stick stationary. Move only the upper stick. Then, with hand half open, rest the lower stick at the base of your thumb and between the top and first joint of your third finger. Next, keeping the lower stick in the same position, hold the upper stick with the top of your right thumb, index finger and third finger in the same way as you hold a pencil. Remember to keep the lower stick in a fixed position and to move only the upper stick.

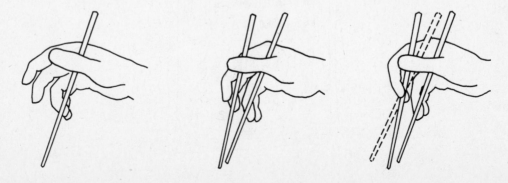

## Model #5   How to Make an Airplane

To make an airplane from a postcard you will need the following materials: one postcard, a ruler, Scotch tape, a ballpoint pen, and scissors.

The first step is to draw three lines across a postcard. The lines should divide the card into four equal parts following A. Then, cut along the lines. One of the parts will be a body. On the first part draw three lines that divide it into four equal parts following B. Then, fold down the sides and tape them following C. Next, another part of A will be a weight. Wind this second part of A around the top of the body and tape it there following D. Next, another part of A will be the front wing. Draw a line down the center of this third part of A and tape it behind the weight following E. The last part of A will be the tail wing. First, cut this last part in half and then draw a line down the center of one of the halves and tape the tail wing to the body following F. Then, turn down the center of the other half and tape the tail fin to the body following F.

After that, try to fly the plane and try to control the flight well.

Good luck!

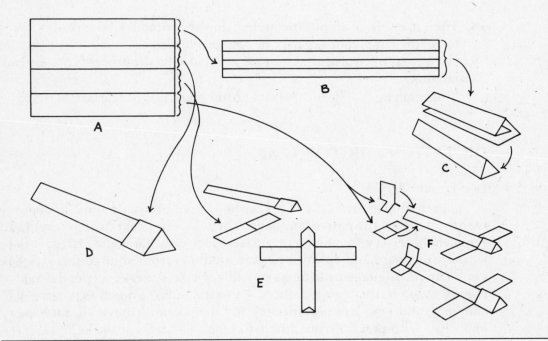

---

## Quotations

Things that we have to learn to do, we learn by doing them.

ARISTOTLE

Whatever is worth doing at all, is worth doing well.

LORD CHESTERFIELD

Knowing how to do a thing is easier than doing it.

ANONYMOUS

## ELEMENTS OF STYLE

### Writing a Process Composition

Exposition is often used to give directions or to tell someone how to do something. This type of composition is called a process composition.

There are certain basic requirements for writing process compositions:

1. Be very clear.
2. Choose a process that you are familiar with and that you have actually done yourself.
3. Give complete details and assume that the reader has not performed the process before.
4. Include negative directions.
5. If necessary, include a sketch or a map to make the instructions easier to understand.
6. Use chronological order.
7. Present the process as a list of numbered steps: 1.
    2.
    3. etc.

8. Then use this as an outline and write the procedures the reader needs to follow simply and clearly in paragraph form.
9. Here are some words that may help you to keep the process composition moving:
    You begin by ... Then ... Next ... After you have ... The last step is to ...

## DICTATION / DICTO-COMP

*How to Learn English*

To learn English, first try to go to the United States or another country where English is the native language. Then find the best possible school and register there. Try to take an intensive course, as that is the fastest way to learn. Study hard and don't sit next to students from your country. Speak your native language as little as possible. Make American friends. Watch television, go to the movies, and listen to the radio as much as possible. Go shopping and read the newspapers and magazines. Above all, take every opportunity to practice your English. Don't be afraid to make mistakes.

## ACTIVITIES

**A.** The sentences below make up a process composition. They are not in correct order. Look at the cues and arrange them in correct order. Then write the sentences in paragraph form. Start the paragraph with the following sentence: "Everyone can build a castle, even if it is only a sand castle."

*How to Build a Sand Castle*

When you have finished the towers, build a moat and a bridge for your castle.

First, get a pail and a shovel.

When you have the water, build a little hill of sand so you have the material for your castle.

The last step is to put a beautiful flag on the top of the highest tower.

Then, choose a flat place on the beach.

Now start building towers from the sand hill.

After you have chosen a spot for your castle, go to the sea and fill the pail with water.

Wet the sand with the sea water to help you form walls and windows in the towers.

Remember: Build sand castles on the beach, not in your everyday life.

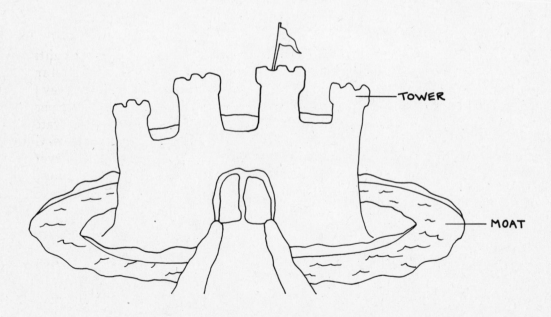

TOWER

MOAT

## COMPOSITION WRITING

**B.** Write a process composition following the model compositions on one of the following topics.

   1. Write a composition giving a recipe.
   2. Write a composition on How to Eat Pizza, How to Bathe a Dog, How to Play a Game or a Sport, How to Prepare for a Test, How to Give First Aid, How to Use a Copy Machine, How to Use a Laundry Machine, How to Choose a Vocation, or anything else. Be careful to choose a subject that is simple and not too broad.

**C.** Giving Directions: Write a composition explaining to a friend how to drive a car from one place to another. Choose a route that involves turns. Be sure to identify landmarks so that your reader will be able to follow your directions. When giving directions:

   1. Choose the easiest route.
   2. Give the directions in the order in which they should be followed.
   3. If possible, name something that is easily seen near the place to be reached.
   4. Be very clear in your directions.

# Model Composition / A Typical Day in My Life

My alarm clock rings at seven o'clock every morning, and I usually get up at once. I jump out of bed and do physical exercises for ten minutes. Then I am ready either to get back into bed or to take a quick cold shower. After my shower, I plug in my electric razor and shave. Then I plug in my electric toothbrush and brush my teeth. Next, I comb my hair, wash my face again, and put on after-shave lotion. After that, I pick out my suit, shirt, and tie for that day. I get dressed, and then I eat breakfast. For breakfast, I usually have grapefruit juice, scrambled eggs, toast, and coffee. After breakfast, I sometimes smoke a cigarette and listen to the news on the radio. At 8:00 A.M., I put on my coat, and I leave for school.

I generally go to school by subway. The subway is always crowded, and I don't often get a seat. In the subway, on my way to school, I look at the signs on the walls of the car, watch the faces of the other passengers, and read the newspaper headlines over someone's shoulder. It takes me about half an hour to get to school. My first class begins at nine o'clock, and my last class ends at three. After school hours, I sometimes go to the Student Center or to a coffee house with my friends for an hour or so. Afterwards, I go home.

As soon as I get home from school, I sit down and do my homework and study my lessons for the next day. At seven o'clock I eat dinner with my brother. Then I relax. Some nights I watch television for an hour or two, read, or write letters. Other nights I listen to my jazz records or work on my stamp collection. Sometimes I take a walk in the evening, or visit a friend, or go out on a date. I usually get home by midnight because by twelve o'clock I am generally rather tired. I take off my clothes, get into bed, and fall asleep immediately. I sleep until the alarm goes off again the next morning.

---

**Quotations**

The happiest part of a man's life is what he passes lying awake
in bed in the morning.
DR. SAMUEL JOHNSON

Life is a merry-go-round.
GEORGE W. CURTIS

# COMPOSITION EXERCISES

## Comprehension Questions on the Model Composition

A. Make believe you are the author of the model composition and answer the following questions in complete sentences.

1. What time does your alarm clock ring?
2. What do you usually do when your alarm clock rings?
3. What do you do for ten minutes after you jump out of bed?
4. What are you ready for then?
5. What do you do after your shower?
6. What do you do after that?
7. What do you do next?
8. What do you pick out after that?
9. What do you usually have for breakfast?
10. What do you sometimes do after breakfast?
11. What time do you leave for school?
12. How do you generally go to school?
13. Do you usually get a seat?
14. What do you do in the subway?
15. How long does it take you to get to school?
16. What time is your first class?
17. What time does your last class end?
18. Where do you sometimes go after school hours?
19. Where do you go afterwards?
20. What do you do as soon as you get home?
21. What time do you eat dinner? With whom do you eat dinner?
22. What do you do after dinner?
23. What do you do some nights?
24. What do you do other nights?
25. What other things do you sometimes do in the evening?
26. What time do you usually get home?
27. How do you feel by twelve o'clock?
28. What do you do when you get home at midnight?
29. Until when do you sleep? (How long do you sleep?)

## Common Expressions and Idioms

*Paragraph I*

to get up
to jump out of bed
to get back into bed
to take a cold shower
to plug in an electrical appliance
to put on
to pick out
to listen to something or someone

to do physical exercises
at once
to be ready for something
to get dressed
to have breakfast
to eat breakfast
to leave for a place

**B.**  1. What time do you usually get up in the morning?
2. Do you jump out of bed immediately?
3. What kind of appliances do you plug in?
4. What do you put on at night?
5. What time do you get ready for bed?
6. What do you put on first when you get dressed?
7. What do you eat for breakfast?
8. What time do you leave for school (or work)?

*Paragraph II*
by subway
to be crowded
to get a seat
to look at someone or something
to read something over someone's shoulder
for an hour or so
to go home

9. How do you go to school?
10. Do you always get a seat in the bus?
11. What time is the bus usually crowded?
12. What do you usually look at in the bus?
13. What time do you go home from school (work)?

*Paragraph III*

| | | |
|---|---|---|
| as soon as | for an hour or two | to get home |
| to sit down | to work on something | to be (rather) tired |
| to do homework | to take a walk | to take off |
| to watch television | to go out on a date | to get into bed |
| | | to fall asleep |
| | | to go off |

14. What do you do as soon as you get up in the morning?
15. When do you do your homework?
16. What do you usually do for an hour or two in the evening?
17. What time do you get home from school?
18. What do you take off first at night?
19. Do you fall asleep immediately?
20. What time does your alarm clock go off in the morning?

## STRUCTURE

### Adverbs of Frequency

| | |
|---|---|
| usually | sometimes |
| generally | never |
| always | often |

Adverbs of frequency usually go before the main verb of the sentence except for the verb "to be."

I *usually* get up at once.
I *generally* go to school by subway.
I don't *often* get a seat in the subway.

**but**

The subway is *always* crowded.
I am *generally* rather tired by twelve o'clock.

Note: For emphasis or for sentence variety, adverbs of frequency are sometimes put at the beginning or at the end of a sentence.

*Sometimes*, I take a walk in the evening.

**C.** Answer the following questions in complete sentences. Use adverbs of frequency.
  1. Are you *ever* late in the morning?
  2. Are you *always* on time?
  3. Do you *generally* eat breakfast at home?
  4. Do you *usually* go out at night?
  5. Do you *sometimes* watch television at night?
  6. Are you *often* tired at night?

**It takes (obj. pronoun) + amount of time to do something.**

It takes me about half an hour to get to school.
It takes him about two hours to do his homework.
It takes me a long time to fall asleep.
It takes them an hour to get to work.
It takes us eight hours to fly from Europe to the United States.

**D.**  1. How long does it take you to get to school?
  2. How long does it take to fly to California from New York?
  3. How long does it take John to do his homework?
  4. How long does it take you to get dressed in the morning?

**Prepositions *by* and *until* in Time Expressions**
  1. *by*
     I usually get home by midnight. (Maybe before, but not later than midnight.)
     I generally get to school *by* nine o'clock.
     He usually finishes his homework *by* ten o'clock.
  2. *until* (indicates the end point of time) (not later than)
     I sleep *until* my alarm goes off again the next morning. (Then, I wake up.)
     He goes to school from nine o'clock *until* three o'clock. (Then, he goes home.)
     He is going to wait for you *until* four o'clock. (Then, he is going to leave.)

## ELEMENTS OF STYLE

The model paragraph "A Typical Day in My Life" is in the narrative style of writing. A narrative tells a story. It is important in narrative writing to show the reader the time relationship between sentences. The order of the composition is chronological. First paragraph: morning; second paragraph: afternoon; third paragraph: evening. To show the sequence of time, adverbials of time are used to link the sentences together. In this composition, the following adverbial expressions of time are used to tie the sentences together:

| | |
|---|---|
| then | after school hours |
| after my shower | afterwards (after that) |
| next | as soon as I get home from school |
| after that | at seven o'clock |
| after breakfast | some nights |
| at 8:00 A.M. | other nights |

**E.** Now look at the following paragraph. Rewrite the paragraph and put in adverbial expressions of time in the blank spaces to tie the sentences together. (Fill in the blanks with the following adverbial expressions of time — *First, After breakfast, Then, Next, After that.*)

I get up at eight o'clock. _____ I wash my face and brush my teeth. _____ I put on my clothes. _____ I eat breakfast. _____ I read the newspaper. _____ I leave my house and go to work.

## ACTIVITIES

**F. Fact Sheet — Daily Schedule for Mr. Hill:** Here is the daily schedule for Mr. Hill. Working with a partner, write a composition about his typical day using adverbial expressions of time. Add any details you wish.

| | |
|---|---|
| 6:00 | Wake up |
| 6:00–6:15 | Jog |
| 6:15–6:45 | Shower, get dressed |
| 6:45–7:15 | Eat breakfast |
| 7:15–7:45 | Read the newspaper |
| 7:45 | Leave for work |
| 9:00–12:00 | Teach English grammar |
| 12:00–1:00 | Lunch |
| 1:00–3:00 | Teach English conversation |
| 3:00–5:00 | Correct papers and prepare lesson for next day |

| | |
|---|---|
| 5:00–6:00 | Eat dinner |
| 6:00–8:00 | Go to computer class |
| 8:00–8:30 | Drive home |
| 8:30–11:00 | Relax with family |
| 11:00 | Go to bed |

## DICTATION / DICTO-COMP

Julia usually gets up at seven o'clock in the morning. She puts on her robe and slippers and goes to the bathroom to take a five-minute, warm shower. After her shower, she picks out her clothes for that day and gets dressed. Then she has breakfast with her husband. After breakfast, she washes her face again and puts on her make-up and combs her hair. At eight o'clock she kisses her husband and leaves for work. She works from nine o'clock to five o'clock.

As soon as she gets home from work, she takes a long bubble bath to relax. It makes her feel good. After her bath, she has dinner with her husband. On Thursday nights she always goes to her oil painting class. She enjoys this class very much. She generally gets to bed by twelve o'clock feeling very tired.

## COMPOSITION WRITING

**G.** Write a composition about "A Typical Day in My Life" following the model composition. First make a three-paragraph outline following the organization of the model composition before you start writing.

# Lesson 10

# My Last Vacation

## COMPOSITION EXERCISES

### Vocabulary of Vacation Activities

| | |
|---|---|
| playing tennis | hiking |
| playing golf | swimming |
| horseback riding | surfing |
| fishing | scuba diving |
| lying in the sun | snorkeling |
| sightseeing | sailing |
| traveling | camping |

**A.** What do you enjoy doing on your vacation?

I enjoy —————————————————.

### Vocabulary and Common Expressions

| | |
|---|---|
| to spend a vacation | a discotheque |
| air-conditioned | off-season |
| to sleep late | outdoors |
| to lie in the sun | out-of-doors } indoors (*opposite*) |

### Questions on Vocabulary and Common Expressions

**B.**  1. Where did you spend your last vacation?
2. Is your apartment air-conditioned?
3. On what days of the week do you usually sleep late?
4. How long do you usually lie in the sun?
5. What kind of dances do you do in a discotheque?
6. What do you like to do indoors?
7. What do you like to do outdoors?

### Quotations

No man needs a vacation so much as the person who has just had one.
ELBERT HUBBARD

Vacations, no matter how long they last, always seem too short.
JEAN GAUTIER

The choice and nature of our holidays is more perhaps than anything in our lives an expression of ourselves.
ALEC WAUGH

## STRUCTURE

### The adverbs *very* and *too*

*Very* is an intensifier which strengthens the degree of the adjective or adverb which follows it.

> The weather was *very* hot, but we went sightseeing.
> The dress is *very* expensive, but I am going to buy it.

*Too* is often used as an intensifier that indicates a high degree which is not acceptable to the speaker.

> The weather was *too* hot. We couldn't go sightseeing.
> The dress is *too* expensive for me to buy. (I can't buy it.)

**C.** Fill in the blanks with the correct intensifiers *too* or *very*.

1. It is _____ warm today. Let's go swimming.

2. The teacher speaks _____ rapidly for me to understand.

3. His paintings were _____ good. Many people bought them.

4. The homework was _____ difficult for me to finish in an hour.

5. I am _____ busy now, but I can talk to you for ten minutes.

6. I am _____ lazy to do anything.

7. John is _____ poor to get married.

### Used to

The expression *used to* plus simple verb expresses the habitual repetition of an action in the past.

> What did you *use to* do on vacation?
> We *used to* sightsee in the morning.
> After dinner we *used to* go dancing in a discotheque.

**D.** Complete the following sentences with the expression *used to*.
What did you use to do when you were a child?
When I was a child, I *used to* drink from a bottle.

_____ play _____

_____ have _____

_____ be _____

_____ like _____

**E.** Give two sentences telling what you used to do in your country.
What did you use to do when you lived in your country?
When I lived in_____, I used to _____

_____

_Lesson_ **11**

# Model Composition / My Classmate

Mr. Sago is one of my classmates. He is a young man of medium height and build, and he is a little on the chubby side. He has curly black hair that is starting to get thin, a round face with a small chin, and a fair complexion. His most outstanding feature is his eyes. They are very dark and alive, with long black lashes, and they seem to be smiling at you all the time. This gives Mr. Sago the appearance of being very good-natured or up to some mischief. On the whole, Mr. Sago is a conservative dresser, and he usually wears a gray or dark-blue suit. His ties, however, are loud. He goes in for vivid colors and abstract prints in his ties. Mr. Sago speaks very quickly but in a soft voice. He has a keen wit and enjoys a good joke. He is a very intelligent student, but he doesn't always pay attention in class. Sometimes he writes letters in class, and sometimes he clicks his ballpoint pen or taps his pencil on the desk. But he soon settles down to work again. Mr. Sago gets along well with the other students, and most of them like him very much.

**Quotation**

A man never reveals his character more vividly than when portraying the character of another.

JEAN PAUL RICHTER

## COMPOSITION EXERCISES

**Comprehension Questions on the Model Composition**

A. Answer in complete sentences.
1. Who is Mr. Sago?
2. How tall is he? Is he thin?
3. What color is his hair?
4. What kind of hair does he have?
5. Describe his face.
6. What is his most outstanding feature?
7. What kind of dresser is Mr. Sago?
8. What kind of ties does he wear?
9. How does he speak?
10. What kind of student is Mr. Sago?
11. What does he sometimes do in class?
12. Does Mr. Sago get along well with the other students?

**Common Expressions and Idioms**

to get thin
to smile at someone
to give someone the appearance of
to be up to some mischief
to go in for
to have a keen wit
to pay attention (to)

to click a ballpoint pen
to tap a pencil
to settle down to something
to get along with someone
on the whole

**B. Questions on Common Expressions:** Answer in complete sentences.

1. Do you always pay attention to the teacher?
2. Who smiles at you during the day?
3. Do you ever click your pen? When?
4. How long does it take you to settle down to work?
5. Do you enjoy a good joke?
6. Is your hair getting thin?
7. Do you go in for the new dances?
8. How do you get along with your teacher?

# STRUCTURE

**Adjectives Used to Describe Mr. Sago in the Model Composition**

1. *One-word adjectives* go before the noun they modify.

   a *young* man
   *curly black* hair
   a *round* face
   *long dark* lashes
   a *fair* complexion
   a *gray* suit
   a *dark-blue* suit

   *abstract* prints
   a *soft* voice
   a *good* joke
   a *keen* wit
   an *intelligent* student
   a *conservative dresser*

2. *Adjective phrases* (preposition plus object noun) go after the noun.

   a man *of medium height and build*
   (noun + adjective phrase)

   a face *with a small chin*
   (noun + adjective phrase)

3. *Adjective clauses* (subject plus verb) go after the noun.
   He has curly black hair *that is starting to get thin*
   (noun + adjective clause)

**Adjectives for Describing People**

*Shape of Face*

round
square
oval

heart-shaped
pear-shaped
dimpled

*Hair*
straight
wavy
curly
bald

brown ⎫
black ⎬ brunette
blonde
auburn (red)

*Eyes*
round
almond-shaped
deep set
widely-spaced
close-together

blue
hazel
green
gray
brown
black
violet

*Eyebrows*
thick
bushy

*Eyelashes*
long/short
thick/thin

*Chin*
small
square
receding
prominent
dimpled

*Lips*
thick/thin
full
soft
tightlipped

*Complexion*
dark
fair
pale
rosy
sallow

*Nose*
straight
hooked
Roman
turned-up
long

*Teeth*
straight
white
even
pearly

buck
false
crooked

*Height*
tall
short
medium-height

*Shoulders*
broad
narrow
sloping

*Figure*
thin
heavy
stout
well-built
curvaceous

hour-glass
slight
long-waisted
short-waisted

*Personality*
sparkling
engaging
charming
dull

aggressive
affectionate
depressive
shy

**C.** Fill in the blanks with adjectives. Use each adjective only once.

*My Dream Man/Woman*

My dream man/woman is _____ feet tall and has a
                                        adj.

_____ figure. His/her face is _____ and
adj.                                      adj.

he/she has _____ hair and _____ eyes
           adj.                       adj.

_____. His/her teeth are _____ and _____
adj. phrase                          adj.                  adj.

_____. He/she has a _____ walk and a _____
                        adj.                          adj.

_____ manner. He/she has a _____ mind and a
adj.                                   adj.

_____ personality. He/she is always _____
adj.                                            adj.

and _____, and he/she makes me feel _____.
    adj.                                        adj.

I know a man/woman like this is hard to find. Do you know anyone
like this?

## ELEMENTS OF STYLE

The model composition is in a descriptive style of composition writing.
The object is to describe the person both physically and characteristically.
When writing a description of people, carefully select the outstanding features or traits that distinguish them from other people. Also, describe what
the people do as well as how they act. Follow the outline for the order of the
composition from general to specific details.

## DICTATION / DICTO-COMP

Ms. André is one of my classmates. She is a tall young woman with dark,
wavy hair that is still in a natural condition and an oval face with a small
chin. Her eyes are brown with long dark lashes. Her most outstanding features are her brilliant eyes and her tender, soft lips. She always looks pleasant and always seems to be in a good humor. She is a very neat and informal
dresser, and she usually wears jeans or a skirt with a blouse or a sweater.
Ms. André has a clever mind and is a good student. She always pays attention in class, but sometimes she cuts class. She speaks slowly and usually
avoids taking part in arguments. Ms. André is on friendly terms with the
other students, and everybody thinks well of her.

# COMPOSITION WRITING

**D.** Write a one-paragraph description of one of your classmates or of a friend. Follow the model composition and the outline below. Be sure that you use adjectives that describe both the physical appearance and the personality of the person. What is the most important impression you want the reader to have of this person? Be sure to keep this in mind when you are describing this person.

*My Classmate*

A. Introductory sentence telling who the person is.

B. Physical description
   1. General statement
   2. Specific physical details of appearance

C. Clothing
   1. General statement of what kind of clothes the person usually wears
   2. Specific description of clothes

D. Personality
   1. General habits and personality
   2. Specific examples of personality traits

E. Concluding sentence
   1. General statement about the person's personality

# Model Composition / A Letter

March 3, 19 _____

Dear Pablo,

   I am sorry I haven't written to you since I left home six months ago, but it has been a busy semester for me. In spite of my heavy work schedule, I have managed to have some fun.

   Since my arrival in Washington, D.C., I have gone on a tour of the city and visited some famous landmarks and tourist spots. I have taken some pictures to prove it, too. I have already visited the Smithsonian Institution and the National Gallery of Art. I have gone on a tour of the White House and seen where the President lives. I have been to the top of the Washington Monument and have visited the Jefferson and Lincoln Memorials. My roommate and I have seen a couple of plays and films at the Kennedy Center for the Performing Arts. I have already eaten in a Vietnamese, a Brazilian, and a Mexican restaurant and have tried different national dishes. I have also spent a lot of money on magazines, books, and art reproductions.

   I still haven't done everything I would like to do before I leave this city. I haven't gone to a symphony concert or to a ballet performance yet. So far, I haven't been to Arlington National Cemetery or taken a boat trip on the Potomac River. However, I intend to do all these things in the near future. I haven't made any new friends up to now, but I hope to meet some soon. The International Festival next month will be a good time to do this.

   Last weekend, I visited the Capitol and sat in one of the sessions of the Senate, which is the upper house of Congress. It was very interesting. Next weekend, some of the other foreign students and I are going to speak before a student group in one of the suburbs. Then we are going to have dinner with some American families. I will tell you all about it in my next letter. Please write soon and tell me what you have been doing.

Your friend,
Maria

---

**Quotation**

A man travels the world over in search of what he needs and returns home to find it.
GEORGE MOORE

## COMPOSITION EXERCISES

### Comprehension Questions on the Model Composition

A. Pretend you are Maria and answer the following questions in complete sentences.

1. Why haven't you written since you left home six months ago?
2. What have you managed to have in spite of your heavy work schedule?
3. Where have you gone since your arrival?
4. What have you visited?
5. What have you and your roommate seen?
6. Where have you already eaten?
7. What have you spent a lot of money on?
8. Have you done everything you want to do before you leave this city?
9. Where haven't you gone yet and where haven't you been yet?
10. What do you intend to do in the near future?
11. Have you made any new friends?
12. When will be a good time for you to meet some new friends?
13. What did you do last weekend?
14. What is the Senate?
15. What did you do there?
16. What are you going to do next weekend?
17. Whom are you going to have dinner with afterwards?

### Vocabulary and Common Expressions

go on a tour of
take pictures of
spend money on
eat in a restaurant
sit in on (one of the sessions)
speak before a group
have coffee (dinner) with someone
a couple of
in spite of }
  despite }

tourist spots
landmarks
art reproductions

B. **Questions on Vocabulary and Common Expressions:** Answer in complete sentences.

1. Have you ever gone on a tour of this city? When did you go on a tour of this city?
2. Have you taken pictures of this city? When did you take pictures? What did you take pictures of?
3. Have you spent a lot of money on clothes? When did you spend a lot of money on clothes? What did you buy?
4. Have you ever eaten in a foreign restaurant? When did you eat in a foreign restaurant? Where did you eat?

5. Have your friends ever sat in on one of your professor's classes? When did they sit in on a class?
6. Have you ever had coffee with your teacher? Whom did you have coffee with yesterday?
7. Have you ever spoken before a group of students? When did you speak before them?
8. In spite of your homesickness, have you enjoyed your stay in this country? (Note that *in spite of* has three words.)
9. Despite your heavy schedule, have you managed to have any fun?
10. Have you seen a couple of books on the table? (Note that *a couple of* also means *a few*.)
11. Name some of the well-known tourist spots in your country.
12. What famous landmark can you see in Paris?
13. Which plays have you seen? Was it easy to get tickets for them?
14. Have you bought any art reproductions? When did you buy them and what did you buy?

# STRUCTURE

## Irregular Verbs in the Model Composition

| Present | Past | Past Participle |
|---|---|---|
| is, are (verb *to be*) | was, were | been |
| leave | left | left |
| make | made | made |
| sit | sat | sat |
| meet | met | met |
| have | had | had |
| tell | told | told |
| take | took | taken |
| eat | ate | eaten |
| speak | spoke | spoken |
| go | went | gone |
| see | saw | seen |
| do | did | done |
| sit | sat | sat |
| write | wrote | written |

*Already* **vs.** *Yet*

Note the use of *already* with the present perfect tense (affirmative statements) and *yet* with the present perfect tense (questions and negative statements).

1. I have *already* seen a couple of Broadway plays, but I haven't been to an opera *yet*.
2. Have you gotten used to the fast pace of life here *yet*?
   No, I haven't adjusted to it *yet*.

## Time expressions Used with Past and Future Tenses

*Present Perfect Tense*

1. *since:*     I haven't heard from my friends *since* last month.
2. *already:*    He has *already* finished his homework.
3. *yet:*     We haven't done our Christmas shopping *yet*.
4. *so far:*    They have enjoyed their stay in this country *so far*.
5. *up to now:*   *Up to now*, I haven't shown you my paintings.

*Past Tense:*

1. *ago:*     Where were you a year *ago*?
2. *last weekend:*  *Last weekend*, we went to an art exhibit.
  *month*
  *year*
  *week*

*Future Time*

1. *soon:*     He is going to finish his book *soon*.
2. *in the near future:* The university will build a new library
          *in the near future*.
3. *next weekend:*  *Next weekend*, we are going to see a basketball game.

*Future Tense Substitutes for Future Time*

1. He *hopes* to finish his book soon.
2. The university *is building* a new library in the near future.
3. Next weekend, we *intend* to see a basketball game.

## Uses of the Present Perfect Tense

1. To show an action that started in the past and continues up to the present. Some of the words and expressions used to show this duration of time are *since, for, so far, up to now, until now, up to the present.*

    He has lived here *for* four years.
    He has worked here *since* 1982.

    We have finished five lessons $\begin{cases} up\ to\ now. \\ so\ far. \\ up\ to\ the\ present. \\ until\ now. \end{cases}$

2. To express an action in the indefinite past that may (or may not) occur again in the future.

    I have been to Paris twice.
    **but**
    I was in Paris last year and the year before that. (*specified time*)

    I have been in Paris many times. (*unspecified time. I may go again in the future.*)
    **but**
    President Kennedy visited Paris many times. (*He is dead so it won't occur again.*)

3. To express an action in the immediate past. The words and expressions used to show this recent past are *just, finally, at last, recently.*

I have $\begin{cases} \textit{just} \\ \textit{finally} \end{cases}$ finished my homework.

I have finished my homework *at last.*
He has *recently* found a new job.

4. To indicate that an action was completed before the moment of speaking. The adverb *already* is used.

Would you like to go to the $\Big\}$ movies?

I have *already* seen that movie.
I have seen that movie *already.*

## Uses of the Simple Past Tense

1. To make statements of fact or opinions about conditions in the past. The past tense denotes definitely completed past time whether a time word is given or not.

Napoleon *lived* in France.
It *was* cold yesterday.

2. The word *ago* requires the use of the past tense.

He arrived a minute *ago.*

C. Working with a partner, write the correct form of the verb in parentheses in each sentence. Use only the present perfect or the simple past tense.

1. She _____ (speak) to her teacher five minutes ago.

2. Where _____ you _____ (go) last night?

3. Mary _____ (eat) in that restaurant many times.

4. I _____ (take) the bus this morning.

5. George _____ (do) his homework already.

6. She _____ (make) three new friends up to now.

7. We _____ (finish) this lesson at last.

8. _____ you _____ (have) any letters from home recently?

9. They _____ (leave) school early yesterday.

10. _____ you _____ (meet) any students from your country since your arrival here?

## Verbs Followed by the Infinitive

Note that these verbs are followed by the infinitive.

1. *manage:* She has *managed to save* some money in spite of the high cost of living here.

2. *intend:* Do you *intend to live* in this country?

3. *hope:* When do you *hope to graduate?*

4. *would like:* What *would* you *like to do* tonight?

I *would like* { to see a movie.
to *go* to the theater.
*to stay* home and watch TV.

What *would* mother *like to do*?
Nothing. She is too tired to move.

**D.** Working with a partner, answer the following questions.

1. How did you manage to find a place to live in this city?
2. What do you intend to study after this course?
3. What would you like to do this weekend?
4. What kind of job do you hope to get in the future?

**E.** Fill in the blank spaces with the correct form of the verb in parentheses.

Dear Kenji,

I _____ (be) very sorry I _____

_____ (write — *negative*) to you since I _____

_____ (leave) home two months ago. I _____

_____ (be) very busy, but I _____ (manage) to

have some fun.

Since my arrival in New York, I _____ (go)

on a tour of this city and _____ (see) many

interesting places. I _____ (visit) the Empire

State Building, Lincoln Center, and the United Nations. I _____

_____ (be) to Greenwich Village and to the top of the World

Trade Center, and I _____ (take) many pic-

tures. My brother and I _____ (see) a few

Broadway plays and new films. We _____ also

_____ (be) to a couple of hockey games and to

the Automobile Show. I _____ (eat) in many

foreign restaurants and _____ (spend) a week-

end with an American family. I _____ (go) to

the Metropolitan Museum and the Whitney Museum and to many art

galleries in SoHo. I _____ (meet) people from

all over the world in my class, and _____

(make) many new friends.

I still _____ (do — *negative*) everything I

would like to do before I leave this city. Next weekend, I _____

_____ (go) to Philadelphia. It_____
(be) my first time there.

   In June, I _____ (drive) across the continent
to San Francisco, stopping at many famous places in the United States
like Yellowstone National Park, the Grand Canyon, and Death Valley.
After that I _____ (be) able to say, "I_____
_____ (see) the United States from East to West." I
_____ (hope) that I _____
(find) the time to write you about my adventures. Please write soon and
tell me what you have been doing.

Your friend,<br>Junchi

## Prepositions *in spite of* and *despite* to Show Opposition

*In spite of* and *despite* mean the same thing. Since they are both prepositions,
they must be followed by an object (noun or pronoun). The prepositional
phrase can come either at the beginning or at the end of the sentence. If it
comes at the beginning of a sentence, it is generally set off by a comma.

**F.** Working with a partner, combine the following sentences with *despite*
and *in spite of*.
.We took a trip. The weather was bad.
We took a trip *despite the bad weather*.
**or**
*Despite the bad weather*, we took a trip.
We took a trip *in spite of the bad weather*.
**or**
*In spite of the bad weather*, we took a trip.

He had a cold. He came to school.
*Despite his cold*, he came to school.
**or**
He came to school *despite his cold*.
*In spite of his cold*, he came to school.
**or**
He came to school *in spite of his cold*.

1. She had a heavy work schedule. She managed to have some fun.

_____

_____

2. He was wealthy. He was unhappy.

_____

_____

3. He had a poor vocabulary. He had a good job.

   _____

   _____

4. The weather was terrible. They went out.

   _____

   _____

5. She had a great love of music. She never went to concerts.

   _____

   _____

## DICTATION / DICTO-COMP

Man has made tremendous technological and scentific progress in the last sixty years. In medicine, he has found a vaccine against yellow fever, polio, and measles. He has been able to transplant a human heart and even an artificial heart. He has discovered an oral contraceptive to help prevent pregnancies and has been able to successfully transplant a human ovum fertilized in vitro. In science and technology, he has produced nylon, the Polaroid camera, and the airplane jet engine. He has invented the electronic computer, the helicopter, the Xerox machine, and robots. He has harnessed atomic and nuclear power. He has put a man into space and even landed a man on the moon. In spite of his great progress in science and technology, man still hasn't learned to live in peace with his fellow men.

## COMPOSITION WRITING

G. Write a letter to a friend following the model composition and the outline.
   I. Introduction
   II. Things I have already done since I got to this country
   III. Things I haven't done yet but hope to do before
   I leave this country
   IV. Things I did and what I will do
   A. What I did last weekend
   B. What I will do next weekend
   C. Concluding Sentence (generalization)

# Model Composition / Bad Habits

Everybody has some personal habits that he or she would like to get rid of, and I am no exception. Eating too much is my number one bad habit. This is a difficult habit to break, and as a result I am always on a diet. Twirling my hair is another bad habit. Whenever I am nervous or uncomfortable, I fall back into this childhood pattern. Whenever I am very tired, I have the bad habit of talking too much and saying foolish things. This habit is something I always regret the next day.

Other people have habits that I don't like either. Students who click their ballpoint pens in class drive me up a wall. People who don't move to the rear of a bus and who block the doors are one of my pet peeves. People who don't put the cap back on a tube of toothpaste are another source of irritation. I find this habit very annoying. Unfortunately, we all do things unconsciously that bother other people, but that is because nobody is perfect.

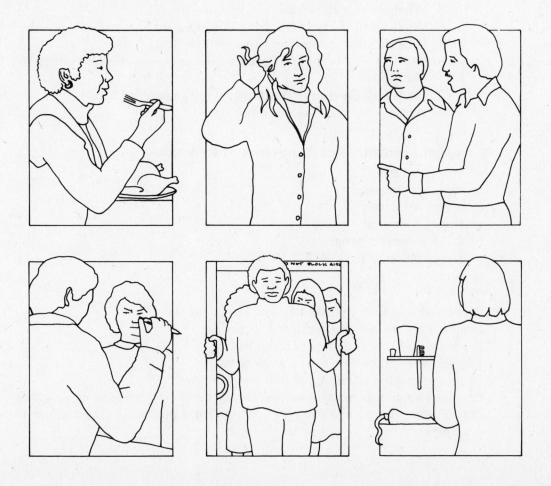

## Quotations

If you want to do something, make a habit of it; if you don't want to do something, refrain from doing it.
EPICTETUS

Nothing is stronger than habit.
ALBIUS TIBULLUS

Habits form a second nature.
JEAN BAPTISTE LAMARCK

# COMPOSITION EXERCISES

## Comprehension Questions on the Model Composition

A. Pretend you are the writer of the model composition and answer the following questions in complete sentences.
   1. Does everyone have bad habits he or she would like to get rid of?
   2. What is your number one bad habit?
   3. What is another bad habit?
   4. When do you do this?
   5. What do you do whenever you are tired?
   6. What kind of students drive you up a wall?
   7. What kind of people in a bus irritate you?
   8. How do you feel about people who leave a tube of toothpaste uncapped?
   9. Do we all do things that bother other people?
   10. Why do we do these things?

## Common Expressions of Annoyance or Irritation

to upset someone
to irritate someone
to bother someone
to annoy someone
to drive someone bananas
to drive someone up a wall
to be ⎫
to have ⎭ a pet peeve

People who talk to themselves out loud *upset me.*
People who can't make decisions *irritate me.*
People who litter the streets *bother me.*
People who smoke in elevators *annoy me.*
People who cut their spaghetti *drive me bananas.*
People who play transistor radios loudly on the street *drive me up a wall.*
People who never have the right change for a bus and hold up a line are a *pet peeve.*

**B.** Answer in complete sentences. Look at the list in Exercise D. You may add to the list.

What kind of people
{
upset you?
irritate you?
bother you?
annoy you?
drive you bananas?
drive you up a wall?
}

What is one of your pet peeves?

**C.** Which of these bad habits do you have? Make sentences with the following pattern using the items below or other items.

*I have the bad habit of* _____ .

winking unconsciously
biting your fingernails
eating too much
chewing gum in public
cracking your gum
cracking your knuckles
leaving doors or drawers open
leaving toothpaste uncapped
having a temper
writing letters but forgetting
    to mail them
being intolerant of other
    people's faults

looking in the mirror all the time
spending too much money
talking too much
telling terrible jokes
smoking too much
drinking too much
forgetting people's names
procrastination
scratching your head, nose, etc.
sniffing
always being late
back seat driving
never putting anything away

**D.** What kind of people bother you? Make sentences with the following pattern using the items below or other items. You may use items from the first list, too.

*People who* _____ *bother me.*

steal the covers in a double bed
sleep diagonally in a double bed
snore
cut spaghetti
play transistor radios on the street very loud
don't move to the rear of the bus
pick their noses
are always late
gnash their teeth
scrape their nails on a blackboard
don't pick up after their dogs
throw cigarette ashes on the floor
use bad language
laugh the loudest at their own jokes
spit
talk to themselves out loud
smoke cigars
talk in their sleep

## STRUCTURE

### Gerunds

Verb forms ending in *-ing* may be used as nouns. When they are used as nouns, they are called *gerunds*.

*Gerund as subject of a verb*
*Eating* too much is a bad habit.
*Twirling* my hair is a bad habit.
*Talking* too much is a bad habit.

*Gerund as object of a preposition*
He has the bad habit *of smoking* too much.
He has the bad habit *of winking* at the wrong time.

E.  Use the gerund form of the verb in the following sentences.
1. _____ (learn) a language takes time.
2. _____ (walk) is good exercise.
3. _____ (smoke) is bad for your health.
4. He is interested in _____ (play) soccer.
5. She is fond of _____ (dance).
6. She is looking forward to _____ (go) to Canada.
7. He is tired of _____ (do) homework.
8. _____(collect) stamps is his favorite hobby.

### Whenever, Wherever, Whichever, Whatever, Whoever, Whomever

*Whenever* — on any occasion, no matter when
*Wherever* — whatever place, at those places
*Whichever* — the one which
*Whatever* — of any sort or degree
*Whoever* — any person who, the person who; used as subject
*Whomever* — any person whom, the person whom; used as object

F.  Fill in the correct word from the above list in the following sentences.
Model: Sit *wherever* you like.
1. I can come at nine or ten o'clock, _____ you will be home.
2. You can have the red one or the blue one, _____ you prefer.
3. I will find you _____ you are.
4. Give the package to _____ you see first.
5. _____ told you that story was lying.

**The relative pronoun** *who*

*Who* is a relative pronoun that introduces an adjective clause in the following sentences. *Who* refers to people and is the subject of the clause.

*Adjective Clause*

Students [who click their pens] annoy me.

*Adjective Clause*

People [who talk to themselves] upset me.

**G.** Working with a partner, combine sentences (a) and (b) into one sentence. Use sentence (b) as the adjective clause.

a. The woman is a lawyer.
b. The woman lives near me.
The woman *who lives near me* is a lawyer.

1. a. The student is intelligent.
   b. The student is from Turkey.

   _____

   _____

2. a. The girl is in my class.
   b. The girl has red hair.

   _____

   _____

3. a. The man is my uncle.
   b. The man is driving the truck.

   _____

   _____

4. a. The teacher spoke very clearly.
   b. The teacher taught me English.

   _____

   _____

5. a. The students passed the test.
   b. The students studied hard.

   _____

   _____

## DICTATION

This is a letter to a newspaper columnist who gives advice.

Dear Abby,

I work in an office with many people. My problem is one co-worker who constantly chews gum in a manner that is very irritating. She is always chewing, popping, and cracking her gum. It continues all day without any consideration for the people working around her.

I don't object to gum chewing if it is done in a ladylike manner, but this person is driving me bananas with her noisy chewing, cracking, and popping. What can I do about it?

Annoyed

## COMPOSITION WRITING

**H.** Write a two-paragraph composition following the model composition about your bad habits and other people's bad habits. First make a two-paragraph outline of the composition you are going to write.

**C.** Change the following imperative sentences to negative form.
Read that book!
*Don't read that book!*

1. Sit next to your friend!

   _____

2. Eat a lot of sweets!

   _____

3. Exercise every day!

   _____

4. Buy an expensive car!

   _____

5. Watch television every day!

   _____

## ACTIVITIES

**D.** Working with a partner, fill in the blanks with the missing correct word. Each blank needs only one word.

Dear Costas,

You have asked me _____ suggestions on how to get along _____ _____ the United States, so I am going to give you some advice.

First, learn all _____ baseball and read the newspapers. Americans love to talk _____ sports and politics. Then, try to go to _____ _____ a baseball game. Americans like to comment _____ the game, the players, and the umpire while they are watching the game. Next, try to watch a parade. There are many parades _____ large cities. People who stand and watch the parades usually talk _____ everyone around. Then, try to stand _____ a line _____ a supermarket, _____ a movie theater, or _____ a school cafeteria. People line up everywhere and often pass the time talking _____ each other. Bring a musical instrument _____ you or get one here. Then go _____ a park _____ a Saturday or a Sunday afternoon and play it. Americans will stop and gather _____ to listen and talk _____ you.

There are some things you shouldn't do. Don't say bad things _____ _____ pets. Americans love pets and won't like it if you are unkind _____ animals. Don't get out _____ line when you want to get _____ a bus or buy a ticket _____ a movie. Americans are orderly about lines. Don't get offended if people call you _____

_____ your first name right away. This is usual here because Americans are very informal, and they just want to be friendly.

That is enough advice for one letter. Just come and I know you will get along.

> Your friend,
> Paul

**Class Activity**

E.   Offer some suggestions of *do's* and *don't* for this country or your own country. List them on the board.

**Other Expressions Useful to Students from Abroad**
Pardon me!
Certainly!
Would you please open the window? Of course.
Would you mind opening the window? Not at all.
Where is (the) <u>bus stop</u>?
What does "<u>breakfast</u>" mean?
Please tell me where to get off.
Congratulations!
Where is the men's room, please?
Where is the ladies' room, please?
My name is _____ .
How do you do?
I am happy to meet you.
Please speak slowly.
Good morning.
Good afternoon.
Good evening.
Good night.
Thank you for a wonderful time.
*Shopping*
I would like to buy this _____ .
How much is it?
How much does this _____ cost?

| *Eating* | *Toasts* |
| --- | --- |
| Waiter! | Cheers! |
| Waitress! | To your health! |
| The check, please. | |

## ELEMENTS OF STYLE

The model composition is a process style of composition. A process composition tells someone how to do something and very often uses imperative form.

## DICTATION / DICTO-COMP

*How to Be a Foreign Student (Humorous)*

It is very difficult to be a foreign student in the United States, but here is some advice that might help you. First, when you do your homework, always write in red ink. That way it will seem that you have fewer mistakes when the teacher corrects your paper. Then, arrive at ten o'clock for a nine o'clock class, and when someone tells you that you are late, tell that person that you are following the time conventions of your country. If there is another student from your country in the class, sit next to him (or her) and speak only in your native language. That way you will be able to communicate easily and not have to bother with English and its strange language rules and pronunciation. When you are asked to write on the blackboard, always start at the very top of the board. If you have a short teacher, you can enjoy watching the teacher jump up and down trying to erase your writing. If the lesson seems long or tiresome, try tapping your foot, cracking your knuckles, or yawning. That will make the teacher almost certainly say, "Take a break!" If none of the above works for you, I am sorry to say that you might have to try to do all the above in reverse.

## COMPOSITION WRITING

E.  Write a letter to a friend giving advice on how to get along in the United States or in your country. Follow the model composition and the following outline.

    I. Introductory Paragraph — State purpose of letter (copy from model). (generalization)
   II. Things to Do (specifics)
     A. Give three suggestions (use imperative).
     B. Explain the reason for each suggestion.
  III. Things Not to Do
     A. Suggest three things not to do (use negative imperative).
     B. Explain why they shouldn't be done.
  IV. Conclusion — Write a final bit of general advice and encouragement to your friend in a closing sentence.

# Model Composition / An Unusual Dream

I don't dream very often, but when I do, I always have unusual dreams. As a matter of fact, I had an extraordinary dream last week.

It was a very beautiful day, and I was on a big ship. The sea was calm and quiet, the sky blue and clear, and the sun warm and bright. Suddenly, heavy clouds covered the sky. The sun disappeared, the wind began to blow, and the sea turned to gray. There was such a fierce storm that the ship almost sank. At that moment another ship appeared from out of the dense fog. It was a pirate ship with a black flag and a crew of armed pirates. The pirates jumped onto our ship, and the battle began. I was assailed by three pirates at once. One pirate had a long beard, the second had a big black mustache, and the third had a wooden leg. I had a sword in my hand, and I fought bravely. All around me a violent battle raged. Soon I was wounded and lay bleeding on the deck. Then, all at once, a very beautiful girl appeared on the other ship. She gave some sharp commands, and all the pirates disappeared. Their ship vanished, too. It seemed to have been gulped down. Immediately the storm stopped and the sun came out again. I was dazzled.

Just then I awoke and found that I was in my own bed. The sun was shining, and there was a ray of light on my face. Perhaps it was that sunbeam that had changed my nightmare into a dream of adventure.

---

**Quotations**

Life and love are all a dream.
ROBERT BURNS

I slept and dreamed that life was beauty.
I woke and found that life was duty.
ELLEN HOOPER

**Song (Round)**

*Row Your Boat*

Row, row, row your boat,
  gently down the stream
Merrily, merrily, merrily, merrily,
  life is but a dream.

## COMPOSITION EXERCISES

### Comprehension Questions on the Model Composition

**A.** Imagine that you are the author of *An Unusual Dream*, and answer in complete sentences.

1. How often do you dream?
2. What kind of dreams do you usually have?
3. What kind of dream did you have last week?
4. Where were you in the dream?
5. What kind of a day was it?
6. What happened to the sky?
7. What happened to the sun, the wind, and the sea?
8. What happened to the ship?
9. What appeared out of the fog?
10. What did the pirate ship have?
11. What did the pirates do?
12. How many pirates attacked you?
13. Describe the pirates.
14. What did you have in your hand?
15. What happened to you?
16. Who appeared on the other ship?
17. What did she do?
18. What happened then?
19. Where were you when you awoke?
20. What was shining on your face?
21. What had changed your nightmare into a dream of adventure?

### Common Expressions

She looked a perfect dream.
I met a dream last night.
I certainly didn't say so; you must have dreamed it.
to awake from a dream
to live in a dream world
to have bad dreams

to dream away $\begin{cases} \text{one's life} \\ \text{one's time} \\ \text{the hours} \end{cases}$

to daydream (*v.*) a daydream (*n.*)
to have a nightmare

## STRUCTURE

### Irregular Verbs in the Model Composition

| Verb | Past Tense |
| --- | --- |
| dream | dreamed, dreamt |
| have | had |
| be | was, were |

| begin | began |
|-------|-------|
| sink  | sank  |
| fight | fought |
| lie   | lay   |
| give  | gave  |
| come  | came  |
| awake | awoke |
| find  | found |

**B.** Fill in the blanks with the correct form of the verb in parentheses. Use the simple past tense.

1. She _____ (give) her husband a tie for his birthday.

2. I _____ (begin) my English lessons last September.

3. They _____ (find) the number in the telephone directory.

4. The *Titanic* _____ (sink) when it hit an iceberg.

5. Napoleon _____ (fight) the British at the Battle of Waterloo.

6. My grandfather _____ (lie) down on the couch for a nap yesterday.

7. The student _____ (dream) she could speak English well.

8. I _____ (awake) at seven o'clock this morning.

9. We _____ (come) to school late this morning.

10. They _____ (have) lunch in the cafeteria yesterday.

### Adverbial Clause of Result

I. such a _____ that _____
      clause (sing. noun)          result

**C.** Combine the following sentences.

There was a fierce storm. The ship almost sank.
*There was such a fierce storm that the ship almost sank.*

1. It was a cold day. I wore two sweaters.

_____

2. He was a good student. He won all the prizes.

_____

3. There was a big crowd. I couldn't see the president.

_____

4. I had a good time. I would like to go again.

_____

II. such _____ that _____
         clause (plural noun or        result
         uncountable noun)

**D.** Combine the following sentences.
There were crowds. We couldn't see the president.
*There were such crowds that we couldn't see the president.*

   1. They were good students. They received "A's" in all their subjects.

   _____

   2. It was good coffee. I drank three cups.

   _____

   3. They were good friends. They never separated.

   _____

   4. There was beauty everywhere. I couldn't believe my eyes.

   _____

III. so _____ that _____
      many/much + adjective or     result
      adverb

**E.** Combine the following sentences using an adverbial clause of result. Follow the example.
It was cold. The water froze.
*It was so cold that the water froze.*

   1. He walked slowly. He arrived late.

   _____

   2. They were tired. They couldn't work any longer.

   _____

   3. The exercises were difficult. I couldn't do them.

   _____

   4. Everything was expensive. I didn't buy anything.

   _____

   5. There were many cars on the road. Traffic moved slowly.

   _____

## ELEMENTS OF STYLE

   1. Use of parallel structures — To express equal ideas in a series, the words must be parallel in form — a series of nouns, of verbs, of adjectives, of similar phrases or clauses, etc.

One pirate had a long beard, the second had a big black mustache, and the third had a wooden leg.

The sea was calm and quiet, the sky blue and clear, and the sun warm and bright.

He was good at painting, designing, and drawing.

2. Use of variety in sentences — This helps make the paragraph more interesting.

   a. Variety in sentence length — Sentences can be either short or long. However, too many short sentences in a string make the reading choppy. A short sentence after a series of long sentences can have a dramatic effect:

   . . . Immediately the storm stopped and the sun came out again. I was dazzled. (dramatic change of emotional effect)

   A long sentence after a series of shorter sentences can have the effect of pulling together all the details into a summarizing or concluding statement.

   . . . Perhaps it was that sunbeam that had changed my nightmare into a dream of adventure.

   b. Variety in sentence movement — The chief way to vary written sentences is to change the order of their parts (or modifiers). Don't use the order of subject-verb-object-modifiers for all sentences. Vary the sentences by putting the modifiers first at times.

   The sea was calm and quiet . . . (subject-verb-predicate adjective)
   Suddenly, heavy clouds covered the sky. (adverb-subject-verbobject)

## ACTIVITIES / STUDENT MODELS

### Student Model #1

It was a night I will remember throughout my whole life. I had gone to bed early, and it wasn't long before I fell asleep. I dreamed that I was flying. I saw the blue sky and the world beneath me. The earth was like a flame, getting smaller and smaller by the second. In a short time I reached a planet whose name I can't remember today. The planet was beautiful. The natural life on it was unbelievable. The planet provided a home for many people, but they didn't resemble earth inhabitants in any way. They were civilized, but the techniques they used were much more advanced than ours. Through gigantic telescopes they were able to see the whole universe. They communicated with each other by television, and they spoke a language that I couldn't understand.

Suddenly, I felt a tap on my shoulder and I woke up. I saw both my children and my husband sitting and watching a movie on television about the faraway planets.

### Verbs with Irregular Past Forms

| *Verb* | *Irregular Past Tense* |
| --- | --- |
| see | saw |
| speak | spoke |
| feel | felt |
| wake up | woke up |
| can | could |

### Student Model #2

I dream every night, but I don't often remember my dreams when I wake up. When I go to bed at night, I sleep very deeply and it is difficult for me to remember the next morning what I dreamed during the night. Sometimes, I can remember things about the last hour of sleep. I remember my dreams very well when I am taking a nap because I am not sleeping deeply then. I also remember when I have a nightmare because I wake up afraid in the middle of the night. I usually have dreams about the people and the things that are around me, and I generally know the persons and the environment of my dreams.

When I was a child, I had a dream about a lion. I dreamed that there was a lion under my bed and that it was trying to eat me, but that it couldn't get out from under the bed. I could hear it scratching the floor with its paws. Sometimes, it pushed the mattress with its head. I was very frightened, but I couldn't move. I don't know why. After many attempts, the lion got out from under the bed and put its paws over the foot of the bed. It was ready to jump on me. This was the moment when I jumped out of the bed very afraid and ran as fast as I could to my parents' room. I opened the door and jumped into their bed shouting, "Daddy, there is a lion in my room!" That night I felt very afraid, and I slept with my father and my mother. I couldn't sleep alone in my room.

### Student Model #3

I don't dream very often, but when I do, I always have unusual dreams. As a matter of fact, I had an extraordinary dream last night.

I was at a party, and I only knew one person there, and that person wasn't near me. He was the host of the party, and he didn't have time to talk only with me. In my dream, a handsome young man came up to me and asked me if I wanted to dance with him. At first I didn't understand anything. I told him that I didn't speak English very well, so he began to speak slowly and clearly. After that, I was able to speak English all during the dream, and I understood everything perfectly. It was wonderful. "I can speak English during the night," I thought, "but now I don't remember what he told me in the dream. However, I do remember that I had a marvelous time last night."

### Student Model #4

I usually dream when I am sick or after I have had a big meal. I always have bad dreams at these times. Once, I had an extraordinary dream.

I was on a high mountain with my friends. The weather was beautiful.

On the top of the other nearby mountains, the last snow was slowly melting. The only noise was the noise made by our own voices. We were happy to spend a couple of hours far away from our noisy office. One of my friends said to me, "Fetch some water from the neighboring river."

I went to get the water and when I came back, my friends had vanished. I was alone and night was near. I was asking myself what I should do when something took me by the shoulders and lifted me into the air. It was a big eagle. It brought me to a strange place where my friends were waiting, frightened. After two minutes, the eagle started to speak. It spoke French to us and said, "If you want to see your homes again, you must answer this question." It began to ask me a question, but I wasn't able to understand what it was saying. It repeated its question twice and then took me and prepared to throw me into a deep abyss. I cried so loud that my sister, who was sleeping in the same room, woke me up and said to me, "You can't stay quiet even at night."

## Student Model #5

It was night, and I was walking in the street. Suddenly, I saw a young man who kept gazing up at the sky and laughing. I realized that he was a drug addict. I went up to him. "What's happened?" I asked him.

"Oh, nothing, nothing," he answered. "It's very beautiful to go into raptures."

The weather was warm, and I sat down near him. His name was Sal, and he was twenty years old. "Why?" I asked him.

"Well," he answered, "the world is very wicked. Some people kill each other. Some people take advantage of others. Some people die of hunger. The innocents pay for the guilty. We have political wars, social wars, and economic wars. There's racial discrimination and inequality of civil rights. We young people don't want this kind of world. We want peace and freedom in all parts of the world. All men are brothers — white, black, and yellow. Only the drug fills me with this sensation of bliss."

"But you're wrong. You're a coward," I replied. "Because you are opposed to the reality of the world, you must act!"

"Sorry, Jack, but some people turn a deaf ear and don't want to change. And I am content with this kind of life, escaping into drugs."

Suddenly, I awoke and looked around. I was alone and I was in my own bed. Then, I understood that I had dreamed it all. Mine was a strange dream. I felt thoughtful and even now, when I think of the dream, I ask myself if Sal was wrong or right.

# DICTATION / DICTO-COMP

*Daydreams*

Daydreams are those thoughts that come into your mind unasked. You are sitting in class and the teacher is talking, but you don't hear a thing because your mind is on something that is going on in your country. You are daydreaming! You are riding on a bus and you miss your stop because you are thinking of how to get enough money to buy a new car. You are daydreaming!

Daydreaming is a universal experience, and most people spend 30 to 40 percent of their waking moments daydreaming. According to a recent study, the leading subject of daydreams among young men is sex. For young women, sexual daydreams occur less often. Females seem to daydream more often than males about problem-solving activities. Problem-solving daydreams are the most common type at all ages.

There are many ways in which daydreams can work to your advantage. Today psychologists believe that daydreaming can help you solve problems, build self-esteem, and prepare for future events.

## COMPOSITION WRITING

**F.** Write a composition on "An Unusual Dream" following the model composition and the outline below. The question outline will help you organize your ideas.

*An Unusual Dream*
I. Your Dreams (generalization)
    A. How often do you dream?
    B. What kind of dreams do you usually have?
    C. Do you dream in color? Do you dream in English?
    D. When did you have an unusual dream?
II. The Unusual Dream (specific)
    A. Where were you in the dream?
    B. Who was with you?
    C. What happened first?
    D. What followed?
    E. What was the conclusion of the dream?
III. Waking Up (generalization)
    A. At what point in the dream did you wake up?
    B. Where were you?
    C. How did you feel?
    D. What did you think of the dream?

## Lesson 16

# Model Composition / My First Day in the United States

I arrived in the United States on February 6, 1983, but I remember my first day here very clearly. My friend was waiting for me when my plane landed at Kennedy Airport at three o'clock in the afternoon. The weather was very cold and it was snowing, but I was too excited to mind. From the airport, my friend and I took a taxi to my hotel. On the way, I saw the skyline of Manhattan for the first time, and I stared in astonishment at the famous skyscrapers and their man-made beauty. My friend helped me unpack at the hotel and then left me because he had to go back to work. He promised to return the next day.

Shortly after my friend had left, I went to a restaurant near the hotel to get something to eat. Because I couldn't speak a word of English, I couldn't tell the waiter what I wanted. I was very upset and started to make some gestures, but the waiter didn't understand me. Finally, I ordered the same thing the man at the next table was eating. After dinner, I started to walk along Broadway until I came to Times Square with its movie theaters, neon lights, and huge crowds of people. I didn't feel tired, so I continued to walk around the city. I wanted to see everything on my first day. I knew it was impossible, but I wanted to try.

When I returned to the hotel, I was exhausted, but I couldn't sleep because I kept hearing the fire and police sirens during the night. I lay awake and thought about New York. It was a very big and interesting city with many tall buildings and big cars, and full of noise and busy people. I also decided right then that I had to learn to speak English.

---

**Quotations**

The first impressions are the most important.
LATIN PROVERB

The entrance hall is the ornament of the house.
UNKNOWN

## COMPOSITION EXERCISES

**Comprehension Questions on the Model Composition**

**A.** Pretend you are the person in the composition, and answer in complete sentences.

1. When did you arrive in the United States?
2. Who was waiting for you?
3. How did you come?
4. Where did your plane land?

5. What was the weather like?
6. Did you mind the snow?
7. How did you get to your hotel?
8. What did you see on the way to your hotel?
9. How did you react?
10. What did your friend help you do at the hotel?
11. Why did your friend leave?
12. What did your friend promise to do?
13. What did you do shortly after your friend had left?
14. What couldn't you tell the waiter? Why not?
15. How did you feel?
16. What did you start to do?
17. What did you finally order?
18. What did you do after dinner?
19. What did you want to see that first day?
20. How did you feel when you returned to the hotel?
21. Why couldn't you sleep?
22. What did you think about New York?
23. What did you decide right then?

## Vocabulary and Common Expressions

| | |
|---|---|
| to wait for someone | to lie awake |
| to take a taxi | to think about |
| on the way | to help someone do something |
| to stare in astonishment at something | to make a gesture |
| | to be upset (adjective) |
| to go back | to upset (verb) |
| to promise to do something | skyline |
| to keep doing something | man-made |
| to be full of | skyscraper |

*Opposites*

| | |
|---|---|
| to land | to take off |
| to unpack | to pack |
| to be impossible | to be possible |

## Questions on Vocabulary and Common Expressions

**B.**  1. Who was waiting for you when you arrived in this country?
2. Do you ever take a taxi to go from one part of the city to another? When do you take a taxi?
3. Whom did you meet on the way to work (school) this morning?
4. What gesture do you make when you are introduced to someone? When do you make gestures?
5. Are you upset when you see an accident?
6. Does noise upset you? (Does the sight of blood upset you?)
7. Is it easier to pack or unpack a suitcase?
8. What time does the plane take off from Orly Airport in Paris? What time does it land in New York?
9. What is the tallest skyscraper in the world?

10. Is it necessary to keep practicing English?
11. Will it be possible for man to live on the moon?
12. What do you usually think about when you are lying awake at night?

## STRUCTURE

### Use of Prepositions of Place and Time

1. *In* a country
   in the United States
   in France
   in Rwanda
   in the Dominican Republic

2. *At* an airport
   at Kennedy Airport
   at Orly Airport

3. *At an exact* time
   at three o'clock
   at 6:15 P.M.
   at nine thirty

4. *In a part* of the day
   in the afternoon
   in the evening
   in the morning

### Use of *Must* and *Have to*

*Must* or *have to* can be used for the present or the future:

| | | |
|---|---|---|
| He *must* leave now. | *or* | He *has to* leave now. |
| He *must* leave tomorrow. | *or* | He *has to* leave tomorrow. |

But: He *had to* leave yesterday.
   He *had to* leave last month.

*Must* can only be expressed by *had to* in the past.

He *has to* go back to work now.   He *had to* go back to work on February 6, 1983.

I *must* learn English soon.   I decided that I *had to* learn English.

### The Use of the Infinitive and Gerund after Verbs

1. Some verbs are followed by an infinitive form.

   He *promised to return* the next day.
   I *started to make* some gestures.
   I *started to walk* along Broadway.
   I *continued to walk* around the city.
   I *wanted to see* everything.
   I *wanted to try*.

2. Some verbs are followed by a gerund.

   I *kept hearing* the fire and police sirens during the night.
   *I *started making* some gestures.
   *I *continued walking* around the city.

*Note: The verbs *start* and *continue* may be followed either by an infinitive or a gerund.

3. Some verbs are followed by a simple infinitive (a verb without *to*).

   He *helped* me *unpack*.

**C.** Answer in complete sentences.
1. What did you promise to do today?
2. What do you want to do tonight?
3. What do you start to do when you are tired?
4. What do you start doing when you are angry?
5. What did you keep doing when you first arrived?
6. What will you continue to do after this semester?
7. What will you continue doing five years from now?
8. Who helps do the dishes in your house?

4. The infinitive is used after *too* + adjective.

I was *too excited to mind.* (I didn't mind.)
He was *too tired to work.* (He couldn't work.)
She felt *too sick to go* to school. (She couldn't go to school.)
They were *too interested to leave.* (They didn't leave.)

**D.** Answer in complete sentences.
1. What are you too busy to do?
2. What are you too tired to do after school?
3. What are you too poor to buy?
4. Are you ever too angry to talk to someone?
5. Is the homework too difficult to do?

### The Past Progressive or Past Continuous Tense

The past progressive or past continuous tense is composed of the past tense of the auxiliary verb *to be* + the *-ing* form of the main verb. It is used to describe a continuous or unfinished action that was going on at some time in the past. (Note: The simple past is used to indicate a completed action in the past.)

| *Continuous action in past* | *Past time* |
| --- | --- |
| My friend *was waiting* for me. | (When my plane landed . . .) |
| It *was snowing.* | (When I arrived . . .) |
| The man at the next table *was eating.* | (While I was in the restaurant . . . *or* When I looked at him . . .) |

**E.** Fill in the correct form of the past progressive tense.

It was very cold and snowy my first day in New York. As I walked along, I looked at everything. Many things _____ (happen) in the city. The traffic _____ (move) along. Policemen _____ (walk) in the streets. Some men _____ (shovel) the snow. Everyone _____ (wear) heavy clothing and boots. Everyone _____ (hurry) and _____ (try) to keep warm.

**Adverbial Clauses**

1. Adverbial Clauses of Time

   My friend was waiting for me *when my plane landed at Kennedy Airport.*
   *Shortly after my friend had left,* I went to a restaurant near the hotel to get something to eat.
   I started to walk along Broadway *until I came to Times Square.*
   *When I returned to the hotel,* I was exhausted.

2. Adverbial Clauses of Reason

   My friend helped me unpack at the hotel and then left me *because he had to go back to work.*
   *Because I couldn't speak a word of English,* I couldn't tell the waiter what I wanted.
   I couldn't sleep *because I kept hearing the fire and police sirens during the night.*

3. Adverbial Clauses of Result

   I didn't feel tired, *so I continued to walk around the city.*
   He felt hungry, *so he went to the restaurant to eat.*

F. Answer the following questions using an adverbial clause beginning with the word in parentheses.
   1. When are you happy? (when)
   2. Why did you come here? (because)
   3. How long did you sleep? (until)
   4. Why did he go to bed early? (Use the clause "so he went to bed early" as the result of the answer to "why.")

## DICTATION / DICTO-COMP (STUDENT MODEL)

I arrived in the United States on March 22, 1983, but I remember my first day here very clearly. Nobody was waiting for me when my plane landed at New Orleans Airport at 7:00 P.M. The weather was warm, and it was very dark outside. I was a little afraid to be in this unknown country, although I was accompanied by my uncle who knew his way about very well. From the airport we took a taxi to the Greyhound Bus Terminal, and on the way I saw many neon lights. There was no traffic at all on the road.

At the terminal, we boarded a bus for New Jersey. The first night on the bus, I slept only two or three hours because I kept thinking about how big the country was and about what I would do here. At first, the language wasn't a problem for me because my uncle was my interpreter. The week after we arrived in New Jersey, however, he went back home and left me alone, so I decided I had to learn the language. Therefore, I worked for a few months and then enrolled in a school and took a course in English.

## COMPOSITION WRITING

**G.**  Write a composition following the model composition and the outline below on one of the following subjects.

*My First Day in (a New Country, City, Job, School)*
I.  Arrival
  A.  When did you arrive?
  B.  Where did you arrive?
  C.  How did you arrive?
  D.  What was the weather like?
  E.  Who came with you?
  F.  How did you feel?
  G.  Who was waiting for you?
II.  The First Day
  A.  What did you see?
  B.  What did you do?
III.  Impressions
  A.  What were your impressions of the (country, city, job, or school)?
  B.  What did you decide (to do)?

# Model Composition / A National Holiday

Thanksgiving Day is always celebrated on the fourth Thursday of November. It is the most traditional of American holidays. The first Thanksgiving was held in Massachusetts in 1621. After a year of great hardship, the Pilgrim colonists wanted to give thanks to God for their first harvest. They invited their Indian friends to join them in a big feast. Today the holiday is still celebrated as a day for giving thanks. It is a day of family reunion, and it is customary to invite friends to share the meal. In some large cities, there are carnival parades for children. In other cities, there are important football games that are played on Thanksgiving Day.

In my family, we always go to my grandmother's house on Thanksgiving Day. All my aunts, uncles, cousins, nephews, and nieces gather for a family homecoming. We always invite some friends to join us. Everyone is glad to see everyone else, and there is a very busy exchange of gossip. Some of us soon disappear into the kitchen to help my grandmother prepare the dinner. Others, meanwhile, settle down to watch a football game on television or to discuss business or politics. If the weather permits, some of the more athletic of us go outside to play ball with the children. At about four o'clock we all sit down to dinner. My grandfather gives thanks for the blessings we have received, and then he starts to carve the turkey. We always have the traditional dinner of stuffed turkey, cranberry sauce, apple cider, sweet potatoes, chestnuts, and pumpkin pie. After dinner, no one can move, and we all sit around and talk, play word games, or tell jokes until it is time to go home. It is always difficult to leave because Thanksgiving Day is one of the few days of the year when the entire family gets together.

---

**Quotations**

With the slothful it is always a holiday.

THEOCRITUS

A perpetual holiday is a good working definition of hell.

GEORGE BERNARD SHAW

## COMPOSITION EXERCISES

### Comprehension Questions on the Model Composition

**A.** Imagine that you are the author of the model composition, and answer in complete sentences.

1. When is Thanksgiving Day celebrated?
2. When was the first Thanksgiving held? Where was it held?
3. Why did the Pilgrims want to give thanks to God?
4. Whom did they invite to join them in a big feast?
5. How is the holiday still celebrated today?

6. What is it customary to do on Thanksgiving Day today?
7. What are there in some large cities?
8. What are there in other cities?
9. Where do you always go on Thanksgiving Day?
10. Who gathers for a family homecoming?
11. Whom do you always invite?
12. What is there a busy exchange of?
13. Where do some of you soon disappear to?
14. Why do you disappear into the kitchen?
15. What do others do, meanwhile?
16. If the weather permits, what do the more athletic of you do?
17. What time do you sit down to dinner?
18. Who gives thanks for the blessings received?
19. Who carves the turkey?
20. What do you always have for Thanksgiving dinner?
21. What happens after dinner?
22. How long do you sit around and talk?
23. Why is it always difficult to leave?

### Vocabulary and Common Expressions

traditional
hardship
harvest
a feast
a family reunion
blessings
to carve

to share
gossip (noun)
to gossip (verb)
to gather
to disappear
to discuss business/
 politics
to sit down to dinner

to give thanks for
 something
to sit around
to get together
a family homecoming
carnival parade
to be customary
football games
to settle down

### Questions on Vocabulary and Common Expressions

B.
1. What is the most traditional holiday in your country? What is the traditional dress in your country?
2. Give an example of a hardship. (It is a hardship [plus infinitive phrase] . . .)
3. When is the harvest season in your country?
4. Do the women in your country discuss business and politics?
5. What time do you usually sit down to dinner?
6. Give an example of a blessing. (It is a blessing [plus infinitive phrase] . . .)
7. To whom do you give thanks for your blessings?
8. Have you ever carved your initials in a tree?
9. Where do you and your classmates get together after class?
10. On what occasions does your family have a reunion?
11. Is it customary to be on time in your country?
12. Whom do you share your apartment with?
13. Who gossips more, men or women?
14. Is it easy or difficult for children to settle down in a classroom?
15. On what holiday do you have a big feast?

# STRUCTURE

## The Passive Voice

The following sentences are in the passive voice. The passive voice is used when the performer of the action is understood and is not important for the statement of the facts in the sentence.

Thanksgiving Day *is* always *celebrated* on the fourth Thursday of November.

The first Thanksgiving *was held* in Massachusetts in 1621.

Important football games *are played* on Thanksgiving Day.

**C.** Answer the following questions in complete sentences using the passive voice.

1. When is Independence Day celebrated in your country?

_____

2. When was the first Independence celebration held in your country?

_____

3. When are the important soccer games played in your country?

_____

## The Use of the Word *Still*

*Still* is an adverb that shows an action that is the same today as it was sometime in the past.

The pilgrims celebrated the first Thanksgiving by giving thanks to God. Today, the holiday is *still* celebrated as a day for giving thanks.

When I was a child, I liked to be outdoors. Today, I *still* like to be outdoors.

My husband started painting as a hobby ten years ago. Today, he *still* paints every weekend.

**D.** What did you do when you were a child that you still do today? (Give five sentences.)

When I was a child, I _____ . Today, I still _____ .

_____

_____

_____

_____

_____

_____

_____

_____

### The Use of the Infinitive Construction

1. The infinitive is used to show reason or purpose.

   Some of us soon disappear into the kitchen *to help my grandmother.* (Why? Reason.)

   Others settle down *to watch a football game on television.*

   Some go outside *to play ball with the children.*

2. The infinitive is used after certain adjectives.

   It is customary *to invite friends.*

   It is always difficult *to leave.*

   Everyone is glad *to see everyone else.*

3. Some verbs are followed by an object plus an infinitive.

   They invited their Indian friends *to join them in a big feast.*

   It is customary to invite friends *to share the meal.*

   We always invited some friends *to join us.*

4. The infinitive is used as an adjectival modifier after a predicate noun.

   It is time *to go home.*

   It is an interesting place *to visit.*

   That is a good thing *to remember.*

5. Some verbs are followed by infinitives.

   The Pilgrim colonists *wanted to give thanks.*

   After he gives thanks, he *starts to carve the turkey.**

*After the verbs *start, begin, continue, hate, like, love,* and *prefer,* either the infinitive or gerund (*-ing*) form may be used.

| | |
|---|---|
| He *started to work* last week. | He *started working* last week. |
| She *continued to study* English. | She *continued studying* English. |
| They *hated to do* homework. | They *hated doing* homework. |
| They *preferred to stay* home. | They *preferred staying* home. |

6. Some verbs are followed by a simple infinitive (without *to*).

   Some of us *help* my grandmother *prepare* the dinner.

E. Answer the following questions using infinitive constructions.

    1. What kind of book is interesting to read?

    2. Why are you studying English?

    3. Why do people save money?

    4. What is everyone happy to have?

    5. What is an interesting city to visit?

    6. What do you want to do after class?

F. Finish the following sentences with infinitive constructions.

    1. Is it unusual _____ ?

    2. Where did you want _____ ?

    3. Tom invited Ellen _____ .

    4. They are studying hard _____ .

    5. She bought a new dress _____ .

    6. The library is a good place _____ .

## DICTATION / DICTO-COMP

Halloween is a spooky holiday. It always falls on the last day of October. Originally it came from a Catholic church holiday to honor all saints, but the holiday customs are of pagan origin. Today in the United States, Halloween is a fun holiday for children and grown-ups. Children dress up in costumes and go from door to door "trick or treating." Grownups give them a treat of candy, cookies, or money. If the children don't get a treat, they will sometimes play a trick on you. On this day it is usual to see children dressed like witches, black cats, devils, and skeletons. Today, American children also collect money for UNICEF* on Halloween. Another custom is to hollow out a pumpkin and make a jack-o'-lantern. The jack-o'-lantern is then placed in the window with a candle inside. Children and grown-ups alike go to masquerade parties in fantasy costumes on this holiday.

*United Nations Children's Fund

## COMPOSITION WRITING

**G.** Write a composition about a holiday in your country following the model composition and the outline.

*A National Holiday*

I. A National Holiday
    A. Which holiday do you think is the most interesting?
    B. When does it occur?
    C. How long does it last?
    D. What does it celebrate?
    E. Why does it occur on that particular date?
    F. What do people do and wear on this holiday?

II. Personal Celebration
    A. How do you celebrate this holiday?
    B. What do you do and wear on this holiday?

# Lesson 18

# Model Composition / An Important Object

When I was a child I had many toys, but the thing I remember best is three yards of gold-colored silk. This was my favorite plaything. My father had brought the material home one day, along with many other things, after one of his trips abroad. When he asked me what I wanted, I chose this piece of silk. Not only was it beautiful to look at, but it was also soft and smooth to touch. The three yards of gold silk and I soon became inseparable. It was my passport into the world of fantasy. With it, I could become any character I had read or heard about by draping and twisting the silk into different costumes. One day I was Cinderella all dressed up for the ball; another day I was Little Red (Gold) Riding Hood; and still another day I was Wonder Woman or someone from another planet. Sometimes I was a bride or a princess, and other times I was a ballet dancer or a famous actress. I was an Indian woman in a sari, a South Sea Islander, and even once an Eskimo. I was anybody I wanted to be.

Today, I can still remember the wonderful sense of escape that it gave me. All my childhood toys and games are long since gone, but somewhere in a box at the bottom of a closet, there is still three yards of gold-colored silk.

---

## Quotations

To love playthings well as a child, to lead an adventurous and honorable youth, and to settle, when the time arrives, into a green and smiling age, is to be a good artist in life and deserve well of yourself and your neighbor.

ROBERT LOUIS STEVENSON

Old boys have their playthings as well as young ones; the difference is only in the price.

BENJAMIN FRANKLIN

## COMPOSITION EXERCISES

### Comprehension Questions on the Model Composition

A.  Pretend you are the author of the model composition, and answer in complete sentences.

   1. What was your favorite plaything when you were a child?
   2. How did you get the material?
   3. Why did you especially like this piece of silk?

4. What could you do with the three yards of silk?
5. How did you become your favorite characters?
6. What fictional characters did you become in your fantasy world?
7. Who else did you become?
8. What is still in the bottom of your closet today?

## Vocabulary and Common Expressions

to remember best                    plaything
to become inseparable               fantasy
to become a character
to dress up
to be dressed up
to get dressed up
to be long since gone

## Questions on Vocabulary and Common Expressions

**B.**  1. What do you remember best about your childhood?
2. Did you ever have a toy or a pet from which you became insepa-rable? What was it?
3. What fictional character did you want to become when you were younger?
4. When do you get dressed up?
5. What was your favorite plaything as a child?
6. What kind of fantasies do you have?
7. Name some things that are long since gone. (e.g., Knights in shin-ing armor are long since gone. Dinosaurs are long since gone.)

## STRUCTURE

### The Past Perfect Tense

The past perfect tense is used to refer to an action in the past that took place before another action in the past. It can only be used in relation to another past action.

**C.**  Before I got to class this morning, I had already done many things. Here are some of the things I had done. (Use past perfect tense.)

1. I _____ (take) a shower.
2. I _____ (make) three telephone calls.
3. I _____ (read) a newspaper.
4. I _____ (write) two letters.
5. I _____ (go) to the supermarket.

**D.** By 9:00 P.M. last night, what had you already done? (Use past perfect tense.)

*By 9:00* P.M. *last night, I had already finished my homework.*

1. _____

2. _____

3. _____

4. _____

5. _____

**E.** Look at the examples below. Then combine the following sentences into one sentence using the past perfect tense and the word in parentheses.

I learned to read at the age of four.

I started school at the age of five.

*I had learned to read before I started school.*

*I started school after I had learned to read.*

*I had learned to read when I started school.*

My husband ate dinner at six.

I got home at eight.

*My husband had already eaten dinner when I got home.*

*My husband had already eaten dinner before I got home.*

*I got home after my husband had already eaten dinner.*

He composed an opera in 1970.

He was thirty in 1972.

*By the age of thirty he had already composed an opera.*

*He had composed an opera before he was thirty.*

1. She graduated from high school in 1982.   (after)
   She came to this country in 1983.

   _____

2. He arrived in class at 9:00 A.M.
   He spoke to someone in the office at 8:30 A.M.   (before)

   _____

3. The class started at 2:00 P.M.
   He did his homework at 1:00 P.M.   (by the time)

   _____

4. She married Tom last year.
   She had two husbands before that time.   (when)

   _____

5. She was twenty-five.
   She had four children.   (before)

   _____

6. The class started at 9:00 A.M.   (when)
   John arrived at 9:30 A.M.

   _____

### Correlative Conjunctions

Sometimes conjunctions are used in pairs to connect two basic sentence patterns or two parallel sentences of any kind. These pairs of conjunctions are called correlative conjunctions. *Not only . . . but* (also) is an example of a correlative conjunction.

> It was beautiful to look at.
> It was soft and smooth to touch.
> *Not only* was it beautiful to look at, *but* it was *also* soft and smooth to touch.
> He attends the university.
> He works every evening.
> *Not only* does he attend the university *but* he *also* works every evening.
> (Notice the question word-order after *not only*.)

**F.** Combine the following pairs of sentences using the correlative conjunction *not only . . . but* (also).

1. He has a degree in medicine.
   He has a degree in law.

   _____

2. He visited eight countries in Europe last summer.
   He visited four countries in Africa.

   _____

3. Mary speaks French and Spanish.
   Mary speaks German and Russian.

   _____

4. My fiancé has a lot of money.
   My fiancé is very handsome.

   _____

## DICTATION / DICTO-COMP

Sometime during their second year of life, many children develop imaginary friends. Some children begin their companionship with these invisible friends as early as two years of age, while others begin later. The friendship may last only a month or two, or it may go on for years. Many children give their companions human qualities. Other children have animals for this imaginary friend. Boys more often have imaginary animals for friends, and girls prefer humans. Some children create these imaginary friends because they are lonely or as a way of expressing feelings. Other children use these companions to transfer blame for wrongdoings. Imaginary friends are usually associated with a lively imagination, and most children outgrow their companions in time.

# COMPOSITION WRITING

**G.** Write a composition about an object that was important to you as a child. Follow the model composition and the outline below as much as possible.

*An Important Object*

I. A Favorite Childhood Object
   A. Description of object
   B. How you got it
   C. What you did with it
   D. Meaning of object to you

II. Present-day Memories
   A. How you feel about the object today
   B. What happened to the object

# Model Composition / Two Friends

Human beings are social animals, and it is in their nature to form friendships. People are very lucky if, among their friends, they have one really close and intimate friend. I have two such friends. Their names are George and Kevin. They both have brown hair and brown eyes and they both have gentle personalities. George is two years older than Kevin and taller and thinner. He is built as straight as an arrow, and his face is longer and more angular than Kevin's. Kevin is shorter but stronger than George and has a fuller and rounder face. Kevin is quieter than George and talks much less than George does. George is more cheerful than Kevin and always tells us jokes and funny stories about his life. He is more experienced in life than Kevin because he has lived a more adventurous life. George is also more impatient than Kevin. George is accustomed to doing everything quickly, from working to talking. Kevin, on the other hand, speaks and works much more slowly. Both of them respect time and are usually early for an appointment.

Both Kevin and George like nature and outdoor sports and are fond of hiking, swimming, and jogging. They are both interested in music, but George prefers country western and rock, while Kevin would rather listen to classical music. In reading, their tastes are similar and they both enjoy reading biographies and books about history. They are both career-oriented, but George wants to be a fashion designer while Kevin wants to be a computer programmer. At times their personalities seem very different, but at other times they seem very much alike. I feel very fortunate all the time, however, to have them both as friends.

---

**Quotations**

Comparison, more than Reality, makes men happy or wretched.
THOMAS FULLER

Nothing is good or bad, but by comparison.
THOMAS FULLER

## COMPOSITION EXERCISES

### Comprehension Questions on the Model Composition

A. Pretend you are the writer of the model composition, and answer in complete sentences.
   1. What kind of animals are human beings?
   2. What are your friends' names?
   3. What color hair and eyes do your friends have?
   4. Who is older?
   5. How is George built?
   6. What kind of face does Kevin have?

7. Who tells jokes and funny stories?
8. Who speaks and works more slowly?
9. How do they both feel about time?
10. What are they both fond of?
11. What are they both interested in?
12. What kind of music does George prefer?
13. What kind of music would Kevin rather listen to?
14. What does George want to be? What does Kevin want to be?
15. Compare their personalities.

## Vocabulary and Common Expressions

to be lucky
to be experienced in life
to live an adventurous life

to be fond of
to be interested in
to prefer
would rather

to be similar
to be different
to be alike
to be career-oriented

## Questions on Vocabulary and Common Expressions

**B.** 1. Do you think you are lucky? Tell us about a lucky incident.
2. Who is more experienced in life, your mother or your father?
3. Who lived an adventurous life? (historical)
   Who is living an adventurous life today?
4. Are you accustomed to the weather in this city?
5. What are you fond of?
6. What sports are you interested in?
7. Would you rather live in the country or in the city?
8. Do you prefer hot weather to cold weather?
9. Are you and your brother (sister) alike or different?
10. Are the people in your country similar to or different from the people in this country? How?
11. Are you career-oriented? What do you want to be?

# STRUCTURE

## Comparatives of Adjectives and Adverbs

1. Comparisons of Inequality of Adjectives and Adverbs
   a. Adjectives and adverbs of one syllable, and of two syllables ending in *ow*, *y*, and *er*, form their comparative form by adding *er*. *Y* is changed to *i* before *er* is added. The word *than* is used in the second part of the comparison.

George is two years *older* than Kevin.
George is *happier* than Kevin.
Kevin is *shorter* than George.
This room is *narrower* than that one.
Alice is a *sweeter* person than Marilyn.

*Note the use of the indefinite article (*a, an*) plus comparative form of adjective plus noun (singular) plus *than*.

b. Adjectives and adverbs of two or more syllables form their comparative form by adding *more* before the word compared. The word *than* is used in the second part of the comparison.

George's face is *more angular* than Kevin's.

Alice is a *more patient* person than Marilyn.

Kevin speaks *more slowly* than George.

2. Comparison of Equality

When two things that are the same are compared, this pattern is used:

as + *adjective* + as

as + *adverb* + as

George is built *as straight as* an arrow.

George isn't *as patient as* Kevin.

My mother drives *as carefully as* my father.

3. Irregular Forms of the Comparative and Superlative

| | *Comparative Degree* | *Superlative Degree* |
|---|---|---|
| good } well } | better | best |
| bad } badly} | worse | worst |
| far | { further { farther | furthest farthest |
| little | less | least |
| much} many} | more | most |

C. Make comparisons of inequality with the adjectives or adverbs in parentheses.

1. Tom is _____ (intelligent) _____ his brother.

2. My sister is _____ (pretty) _____ I.

3. My father is _____ (heavy) _____ my mother.

4. New York is _____ (big) _____ that city.

5. He feels _____ (bad) today _____ he did yesterday.

6. Tokyo has _____ (many) people _____ London.

7. This room is _____ (big) _____ that room.

8. The food in my country is _____ (good) _____ the food here.

**D.** Make comparisons of equality using *as . . . as.*

1. Today's lesson is _____ (difficult) _____
   yesterday's.

2. Jane sings _____ (well) _____ her
   sister.

3. Robert is _____ (tall) _____
   Thomas.

4. He spoke _____ (rapidly) _____
   an engine.

5. Are you _____ (rich) _____ Rock-
   efeller?

## Superlatives of Adjectives and Adverbs

1. Adjectives and adverbs of one syllable and of two syllables ending in *ow, y,* and *er* add *-est* to form the superlative. *Y* is changed to *i* before the ending is added. The word *the* or a possessive adjective or noun precedes the adjective or adverb.

   Mount Everest is *the highest* mountain in the world.
   The Sears Building in Chicago is *the tallest* building in the world.
   Tom is *my oldest* brother.

2. Most adjectives of two syllables and all adjectives and adverbs of three or more syllables add *the most* in front of the adjective or adverb to form the superlative.

   The President has *the most difficult* job in the United States.
   He was *the most intelligent* student in the class.

3. The expression *one of the* is used with the superlative plus a plural noun.

   Paris is *one of the* most beautiful cities in the world.
   Einstein was *one of the* most famous scientists in this century.

**E.** Use the superlative form of the adjective or adverb given in each sentence.

1. Robert studied _____ (hard) of all the
   students.

2. He got _____ (good) grade in the class.

3. She bought _____ (expensive) coat in
   the store.

4. Rhode Island is _____ (small) state in the
   United States.

5. Caroline is my _____ (old) sister.

6. This class is _____ (easy) of all.

7. I have _____ (little) money of all.

8. She is _____ (intelligent) student in the class.

9. This is _____ (comfortable) chair in the room.

10. Lincoln was one of the _____ (famous) presidents.

**F.** Working with a partner, fill in the blanks with the correct superlative form of the adjective in parentheses.

Alaska is _____ (large) state in the United States, but it is _____ (little) populated of all the states. It is the northernmost state in the Union and the part of North America _____ (close) to Asia. Juneau, its capital, covers 3,108 square miles and is the nation's _____ (large) city in area. Mount McKinley (20,320 feet) is _____ (high) peak in the United States. Alaska has some of _____ _____ (beautiful) scenery in the United States and _____ _____ (active) volcanoes.

For many years gold was _____ (important) mining product. Then, in 1968, two oil companies made one of the _____ (great) oil discoveries of all time on the Arctic Coastal Plain. Engineers believe this oil field may be _____ _____ (large) in North America. Today, oil is the state's _____ (valuable) mineral product. Fish products are Alaska's _____ (important) manufacturing industry.

## Use of the Gerund Form of the Verb after Prepositions

The gerund is the *-ing* form of a verb used as a noun. If a verb follows a preposition, the verb is always in the gerund form.

He is accustomed to *doing* everything carefully.
They are fond of *walking, gardening,* and *swimming.*
They are interested in *reading.*
They never get tired of *listening* to classical music.
They are in agreement on *having* a party.
My parents didn't believe in *punishing* a child physically.

**G.** Answer the following questions using the gerund form of the verb after the preposition.
1. What were you accustomed to doing in your country?
2. What activities are you fond of?
3. What are most children interested in doing?
4. What kind of books are you fond of reading?
5. What do you get tired of doing every day?
6. What was the class in agreement on doing?
7. What do your parents believe in doing?
8. What don't you believe in doing?

**The Use of** *Would rather* **and** *Prefer*

The expression *would rather plus simple verb* means *to prefer*. It usually refers to present or future time.

The bride *prefers to have* a big wedding.
The bride *would rather have* a big wedding.
The groom *prefers to have* a small wedding.
The groom *would rather have* a small wedding.

**H.** Change the following sentences to use the expression *would rather*.
1. I prefer to have ice cream for dessert.
2. He prefers to live in a warm climate.
3. Mrs. Brown prefers to eat in a French restaurant.
4. They prefer to own a big car.
5. Many men prefer not to marry at an early age.

# DICTATION / DICTO-COMP

*Two Sisters (Student Model)*

I have two sisters who are very different even though they have the same parents. Both of my sisters have brown eyes and both have gay voices and interesting personalities. My sister Marilyn is four years older than my sister Alice and taller and thinner. Marilyn has short brown hair and wears more casual clothes than Alice. My sister Alice is shorter and has a fuller figure. She has long red hair and wears glasses. She is a sweeter and more patient person than my sister Marilyn. Marilyn is smarter and more interested in cultural things than Alice. She is interested in studying to become an architect, traveling throughout the world, and listening to everyone and looking at everything. My sister Alice is quieter and more of a homebody. If it were possible, she would stay at home rather than go out to work.

Both of my sisters like nature and the outdoors, but my sister Marilyn is fond of swimming, skiing, and climbing mountains, while my sister Alice is fond of walking, gardening, and having picnics on the grass. They are both interested in music, but my sister Marilyn prefers jazz and symphonic music, while Alice prefers grand opera, folk ballads, and romantic songs. Most of the time they are in agreement on the political situation, but sometimes they argue about something and then my house becomes very noisy.

My sister Marilyn believes in having a career, in doing interesting work, and in loving others with discretion, but my sister Alice believes in having a home and a family, and in loving others without any conditions. My sisters' personalities are very different. The only thing about them that is the same is that neither one of them is ever on time for any kind of appointment.

## COMPOSITION WRITING

I. Write a composition comparing two people — friends, siblings, or relatives — for differences and similarities using comparisons of equality and inequality. Follow the model composition and the outline.

*Two Friends*

I. Description and Characteristics
   A. General statement of introduction
   B. Physical description
      1. Similarities
      2. Differences
   C. Personality characteristics
      1. Similarities
      2. Differences

II. Tastes
   A. What they are interested in doing
   B. What they are fond of doing
   C. What they are accustomed to doing
   D. Concluding general statement

# Lesson 20

# A Wedding

## COMPOSITION EXERCISES

### Vocabulary and Common Expressions

| | |
|---|---|
| bride | groom |
| maid or matron of honor | best man |
| bridesmaids | ushers |
| bridal shower | bachelor dinner |
| bridal gown | cutaway |
| veil | tuxedo |
| to date | matchmaker |
| to get engaged | wedding |
| to get married | wedding reception |
| wedding presents | trousseau |
| | honeymoon |

### Questions on Vocabulary and Common Expressions

A.
1. Who is usually the best man at a wedding?
2. At what age do young men and women start to date in your country?
3. Is it customary to get engaged before getting married in your country?
4. How long does an engagement last?
5. Are matchmakers used in your country? When?
6. What kind of people are the matchmakers usually?
7. Who pays for the wedding reception?
8. Do people throw anything at the bride and groom in your country? What do they throw?
9. What does the bride's trousseau usually contain?
10. What are the customary wedding presents in your country?

### Quotations

Bridesmaids may soon be brides; one wedding brings on another.
C.H. SPURGEON

A woman is more desirous to be married than a man desires to marry.
BABYLONIAN PROVERB

Marriages are made in heaven.
MIDRASH

If you are afraid of loneliness, don't marry.
CHEKHOV

I have always thought that every woman should marry, and no man.
BENJAMIN DISRAELI

A man who marries a woman to educate her falls into the same fallacy as the woman who marries a man to reform him.
E. HUBBARD

## STRUCTURE

### Adjective Clauses

An adjective clause is a dependent clause that acts like an adjective. It tells you about a noun or a pronoun. It is usually introduced by the relative pronouns *who, whom, whose, which,* and *that.* It follows the noun that it modifies.

When the relative pronoun is the subject of the adjective clause, *who* refers to persons, *which* refers to things, and *that* refers to either persons or things.

> The bride wore a white dress *that was made of silk.*
> The judge *who married them* was a friend of the family.
> Everyone enjoyed the reception *which lasted for four hours.*

When the relative pronoun is the object of the adjective clause, *whom* refers to persons, *which* refers to things, and *that* refers to persons or things.

> The man *whom you met* married my cousin.
> My sister caught the bouquet *which the bride threw.*
> The invitations *that they sent* were delivered late.

When the relative pronoun is the object of the adjective clause, it may be omitted.

> The man *you met* married my cousin.
> My sister caught the bouquet *the bride threw.*
> The invitations *they sent* were delivered late.

The relative pronoun *whose* designates a possessive and can modify the subject or the object of the adjective clause. *Whose* can refer to people or things.

> She married a man *whose brother lives near me.*
> We were introduced to the man *whose son she married.*
> The tree *whose leaves are turning red* is an oak.

The subordinating conjunctions *when, where,* and *why* can also introduce adjective clauses.

> The church *where they got married* was in her hometown.
> I don't know the reason *why they waited so long.*
> Rome is the city *where he was born.*

**B.** Fill in the blank spaces with the correct word — *who, whom, whose, which, when, where.*

1. The bridesmaid _____ catches the bridal bouquet is the next one to get married.

2. The ushers _____ the groom chose were all close friends.

3. The man _____ son she married was born in Italy.

4. Paris is the city _____ they went on their honeymoon.

5. There were many guests at the reception, _____ was held in the bride's home.

6. The table _____ they sat was decorated with flowers.

7. The photographer _____ took the pictures asked everyone to smile.

8. The wedding _____ we attended took place last week.

9. The guest _____ arrived late missed the wedding ceremony.

10. June is the month _____ many people get married.

## Adverbial Clauses of Time

An adverbial clause is a dependent clause that acts like an adverb. It can modify a verb and tell you *time*. Adverbial clauses of time are introduced by the subordinating conjunctions (connectives) *when, whenever, while, after, before, until, since*. An adverbial clause of time can come at the end of a sentence or the beginning of a sentence. When the adverbial clause of time precedes the main clause, it is set off by a comma.

They danced *until it was time to leave.*
*After the ceremony,* there was a big reception.
*When the orchestra started to play,* the bride and groom danced first.
*While they were dancing,* the guests watched and applauded.
*Before she left,* the bride threw her bouquet.
My mother cries *whenever she goes to a wedding.*
They have known each other *since they were children.*

When the verb in the main clause is in the future, the verb in the time clause is usually in the present tense.

I will wait here *until he arrives.*
I will tell him the news *when I see him.*
*After she graduates from college,* she is going to get married.

C. Working with a partner, complete the following sentences with an adverbial clause of time. Remember that your clause must have a subject and a verb.

1. I didn't know any English before _____

2. They will leave when _____

3. We went to the movies whenever _____

4. I always do my homework before _____

5. Tom was watching television while _____

6. When _____, please turn off the lights.

7. After _____ , he went to college.

8. Please don't leave until _____

9. They got married after _____

10. They haven't seen each other since _____

## DICTATION / DICTO-COMP

Americans seem to be going back to the patterns of their great-grand-parents, postponing marriage in favor of an education and a career. Back in the early 1900's, men and women both married at older ages. Then there followed a period when they married younger and younger. According to a survey taken in March 1982, the typical American male was 25.2 years old before getting married for the first time. For women, the median age was 22.5 for a first marriage. Not since 1910 had men waited that long to marry. Women hadn't delayed marriage to that age in this century.

While both men and women are marrying later in life, the number of unmarried-couple households has more than quadrupled since 1970. That, however, is still only 4 percent of all couples.

from the study "Marital Status and Living Arrangements: March 1982" (U.S. Census Bureau)

## ACTIVITIES

**D.** Describe a wedding you went to. Tell one of your classmates about it using the following questions as a guide.

*A Wedding*
1. Who got married?
2. How old were the bride and groom?
3. How long did they know each other before they got married?
4. Who paid for the wedding?
5. What did the bride and groom wear?
6. Describe the wedding.
   a. Who married the bride and groom?
   b. How many guests attended the wedding?
   c. What did they serve at the wedding?
   d. Was there any music and dancing?
7. What kind of presents did the bride and groom receive?
8. Where did they go on a honeymoon?
9. Where did they plan to live afterwards?

## COMPOSITION WRITING

**E.** Now write a composition about the wedding using the above questions as a guide.

# Model Composition / The Ideal Teacher

The ideal teacher may be young or old, tall or short, fat or thin. She should know her subject, but she can make mistakes if she is willing to learn. Her personality is as important as her scholarship. The ideal teacher must be enthusiastic. She must never teach anything she is not interested in. She should be a bit of an actress, and she shouldn't be afraid to show her feelings and express her likes and dislikes. She must like her students and respect them, but she must also respect herself and take pride in her work. Otherwise, she cannot respect her students. The ideal teacher should have an understanding of her students and be able to relate to them. She should be kind, encouraging, and helpful, and she should motivate her students to want to learn. The ideal teacher should see her students as individuals and acknowledge their differences. She must know how to encourage the self-development and growth of each of her students. The ideal teacher is one who grows, learns, and improves herself along with her students.

---

**Quotations**

An ideal is something which ought to be, as distinguished from what is.

JOHN GROTE

Our ideals are our better selves.

A.B. ALCOTT

## COMPOSITION EXERCISES

**Comprehension Questions on the Model Composition**

**A.**  1. What may the ideal teacher be?
   2. What should she know?
   3. May she make mistakes?
   4. What must the ideal teacher be?
   5. What must she never teach?
   6. What shouldn't the ideal teacher be afraid to show and express?
   7. How must she feel about her students?
   8. What else should the ideal teacher be?
   9. How should she see her students?
   10. What must she know how to do?
   11. What kind of person is the ideal teacher?

**Vocabulary and Common Expressions**

to make mistakes
to be willing to do something

scholarship
enthusiastic (adjective)

enthusiasm (noun)
to show one's feelings
to take pride in something

to relate to someone
to motivate someone to do something
to acknowledge differences

### Questions on Vocabulary and Common Expressions

B.
1. When do you usually make mistakes?
2. Are you an enthusiastic person? Do you show your enthusiasm?
3. In your culture is it permissible to show your feelings in public?
4. What do you take pride in?
5. Is it easy or difficult for you to relate to your classmates?
6. What motivated you to study English?

## STRUCTURE

## The Modal Auxiliaries

| Modal Auxiliaries* | Meaning | Example |
|---|---|---|
| can | ability | I *can* swim well.<br>*Can* you dance?<br>I *can't* sing. |
| may | permission | You *may* type your homework.<br>*May* I see Dr. Bonino? |
|  | possibility | The teacher *may* be young or old.<br>It *may* rain tonight.<br>They *may* be late for dinner.<br>I *may* not be here tomorrow. |
| should | duty or obligation | The teacher *should* understand her students.<br>She *should* be kind.<br>She *shouldn't* be afraid to show her feelings. |
| must | necessity | The ideal teacher *must* be enthusiastic.<br>He *must* like his students and respect them. |

*Please note that the above modals are followed by the simple verb form.

C. Answer the following in complete sentences.
1. What languages can you speak? (ability)
2. When may you speak in class? (permission)
3. What should a good mother do? (obligation)
4. What shouldn't a child do? (negative obligation)
5. How old must you be in order to vote in your country? (necessity)

D. 1. Give two sentences telling what you can do. (ability)
2. Give two sentences telling what you may do tomorrow. (possibility)
3. Give two sentences telling what you should or shouldn't do. (duty or obligation)
4. Give two sentences telling what you must do this week. (necessity)

## ACTIVITIES

E. Working in pairs, make believe your son or daughter is going abroad to study. Make a list of ten sentences giving your son or daughter advice. Try to use different modals.

*You must write twice a week.*
*You mustn't go out alone at night.*

F. Divide into two groups. One group will be all female and the other group will be all male. The men will write a group composition on "The Ideal Wife" using modals. The women will write a group composition on "The Ideal Husband" using modals.

When the two groups are finished, someone from each group will write their composition on the blackboard for the whole class to read and compare.

## DICTATION / DICTO-COMP

The ideal student may be young or old, an American or a foreign student. He should be motivated, curious, and disciplined in his work habits. He should have a thirst for knowledge and be prepared to learn, as that is his goal as a student. He can make mistakes, but he must be ready to learn from his mistakes. He should respect his teachers even though he may disagree with them. The ideal student must be willing to listen to all sides of a question. He must be able to think for himself and to form his own opinions. He should be himself and not be afraid to express his ideas or feelings. The ideal student should have a definite goal in life and direct himself towards it. He mustn't get discouraged easily. The time for him to begin preparing himself for a successful future is now.

## COMPOSITION WRITING

**G.** Write a composition in paragraph form about "An Ideal Leader (Parent, Friend, Wife, Husband, Doctor, Pet, Son, Daughter, etc.)."

*The Ideal Leader*
A. What may or can the ideal _____ be or do?
B. What can't the ideal _____ be or do?
C. What should the ideal _____ be or do?
D. What shouldn't the ideal _____ be or do?
E. What must the ideal _____ be or do?
F. What mustn't the ideal _____ be or do?

# Model Composition / My First Flight

Last summer, I took my first airplane flight from Zurich to Chicago. I boarded the plane at Kloten Airport and, from that moment on, my life was arranged for me on the trip. First, I was directed to my seat by the flight attendant. Then, when the plane was ready to take off, the other passengers and I were told to fasten our seat belts. A few minutes after take-off, magazines and newspapers were passed out. Because my ears hurt, I was given some gum to chew. Next, the passengers were given instructions on what to do in case of an emergency. We were all given earphones to listen to music and told that a movie would be shown after dinner. Before dinner, we were asked if we wanted a cocktail. Dinner was served on a tray, but it was attractive and delicious. We were permitted to have a refill on any beverage. After dinner, we were shown a new Hollywood movie. When I felt cold, I was given a blanket and when I felt airsick, I was given a paper bag. Everything was done for the comfort of the passengers. When the plane landed, I was almost sorry to get off and have to start doing things for myself again.

## Quotations

When I was a student in college, just flying an airplane seemed a dream. But that dream turned into reality.

> CHARLES A. LINDBERGH
> (first man to fly across the Atlantic solo)

I could have gone on flying through space forever.

> MAJOR YURI GAGARIN
> (describing in ecstatic terms his flight as the first man in space — April 14, 1961)

## COMPOSITION EXERCISES

### Comprehension Questions on the Model Composition

A.  Imagine that you are the writer of the model composition, and answer in complete sentences using the passive voice wherever possible.

1. When did you take your first airplane flight?
2. Where did you fly?
3. Where did you board the plane?
4. Who directed you to your seat?
5. What was distributed a few minutes after take-off?
6. Why were you given some gum to chew? What happened next?
7. What were you asked before dinner?
8. How was dinner served? What happened after dinner?
9. What were you given when you felt cold? when you felt airsick?
10. Why were you sorry when the plane landed?

## Vocabulary and Common Expressions

| | |
|---|---|
| to fly (verb) — flight (noun) | an emergency |
| to take off (verb) — take-off (noun) | a tray |
| flight attendant | a refill |
| to board a plane | to feel cold |
| from that moment on | to feel airsick |
| to fasten a seat belt | to be sorry |
| to chew | to land — to take off (opposite) |

## Questions on Vocabulary and Common Expressions

**B.**
1. When did you take your first flight? Where did the plane take off from?
2. When do you fasten your seat belts in an airplane?
3. Do children in your country chew gum?
4. Whom do you call in an emergency?
5. Have you ever been airsick? (When?)
6. Who greets you when you board a plane?
7. Were you sorry to leave home?
8. What do you put your dishes on in a cafeteria?

# STRUCTURE

## Passive and Active Voice

Active Voice — *the subject performs the action.*
Passive Voice — *the subject receives the action.*

The Passive Voice is used when the receptor is more important than the performer.

The United Nations was started in 1945.
Tom was run over by a car.

| *Active Voice* | *Passive Voice* |
|---|---|
| Subject + Verb + Object | Subject + Auxiliary (to be) + Past Participle + Agent* |
| 1. Many people read *The New York Times.* | *The New York Times* is read by many people. |
| 2. John wrote the letter yesterday. | The letter was written by John yesterday. |
| 3. Fifty-one countries formed the United Nations in 1945. | The United Nations was formed in 1945. |
| 4. The flight attendants are serving lunch now. | Lunch is being served by the flight attendants now. |
| 5. Many people have visited the Louvre. | The Louvre has been visited by many people. |

| | |
|---|---|
| 6. The President will make the announcement tonight. | The announcement will be made by the President tonight. |
| 7. They are going to do the work at noon. | The work is going to be done by them at noon. |
| 8. He can see the movie later. | The movie can be seen by him later. |
| 9. You must do the work. | The work must be done by you. |
| 10. He had to do the work. | The work had to be done by him. |
| 11. Everyone should study English. | English should be studied by everyone. |
| 12. They told us that they would show a movie. | We were told that a movie would be shown. |

*The agent (*by* . . . ) may be omitted when this information isn't important.

**C.** Use the correct voice (active or passive) and the correct tense of the verb in each sentence.

1. Columbus _____ (discover) America in 1492.

2. America _____ (discover) in 1492.

3. That house _____ (build) last year.

4. English _____ (teach) in all secondary schools next year.

5. Dinner _____ (serve) now.

6. Mr. Brown _____ (teach) English since 1962.

**D.** Change the following sentences from passive to active voice. Note: If there is no agent you must supply one as the subject in the active voice.

1. First I was directed to my seat by the flight attendant.
2. We were told to fasten our seat belts.
3. A few minutes after take-off, magazines and newspapers were distributed.
4. I was given some gum to chew because my ears hurt.
5. We were given instructions on what to do in case of an emergency.
6. We were given earphones to listen to music.
7. We were told that a movie would be shown after dinner.
8. Before dinner, we were asked if we wanted a cocktail.
9. After dinner, we were shown a new Hollywood movie.
10. When I was cold, I was given a blanket.
11. When I felt airsick, I was given a paper bag.

## ACTIVITIES

E. Working in groups, write a paragraph about the life of a baby. Think back to the time you were a baby and everything was done for you. Start the paragraph with the following sentence:

When I was a baby, my life was easy because everything was done for me.

1. What was done for you in the morning and afternoon?
2. What happened when you cried?
3. What happened when you were hungry?
4. What was done for you at night?

## DICTATION / DICTO-COMP

*My Stay in the Hospital*

Last year, I broke my ankle while skiing and spent five days in the hospital. I remember those five days as a time when everything was done for me. First, I was taken to the hospital by an ambulance, and my ankle was set. I was put to bed in a private room and told to ring a bell if I needed anything. Every morning, I was awakened at 6:30 A.M. and washed by a nurse. At 7:00 A.M., my breakfast was served to me in bed. After breakfast, I was taken off the bed and put in a chair while my bed was being made. In the middle of the morning, I was visited by my doctor, who looked at my ankle and asked me how I felt. On the second day, I was taught how to use crutches and given instructions in walking. When I wanted to read, my bed was raised. At night, when I was ready to go to sleep, I was given some medication, and my bed was lowered. After five days, I was released from the hospital. I was glad to get out, even though it meant doing everything for myself again.

## COMPOSITION WRITING

F. Write a one-paragraph composition about the changes that have been made in your city or country in the last twenty-five years.
*or*
Write a composition about the changes you think will be made in your city or country in the future.

Use the passive voice and outline your paragraph first. (In order to help you organize your composition, first make a list of all the changes that have been made or that you think will be made in your city or country.)

# Model Composition / Abraham Lincoln

Abraham Lincoln was born in a log cabin in Kentucky on February 12, 1809. When he was a small boy, his family moved to the frontier of Indiana. Here, his mother taught him to read and write. Lincoln had very little formal education, but he became one of the best-educated men of the Great West.

When Lincoln was a young man, his family moved to the new state of Illinois. Lincoln had to earn a living at an early age, but in his leisure time he studied law. He soon became one of the best-known lawyers in the state capital, Springfield, Illinois. It was here that Lincoln became famous for his debates with Stephen A. Douglas on the subject of slavery.

In 1860, Lincoln was elected President of the United States. He was the candidate of the new Republican Party. This party opposed the creation of new slave states. Soon after Lincoln's election, some of the Southern states withdrew from the Union and set up the Confederate States of America. This action brought on the terrible Civil War which lasted from 1861 to 1865.

On January 1, 1863, during the war, Lincoln issued his famous Emancipation Proclamation. In this document, Lincoln proclaimed that all the slaves in the seceding states were to be free as of that date. In 1865, after the war ended, the Thirteenth Amendment was added to the Constitution of the United States. This amendment put an end to slavery everywhere in the United States.

Early in 1865, the Civil War came to an end with the defeat of the South by the North. Only a few days after the end of the war, Lincoln was shot by an actor named John Wilkes Booth. The President died on April 14, 1865. In his death, the world lost one of the greatest men of all time.

---

**Quotation**

There is properly no history, only biography.

RALPH WALDO EMERSON

## COMPOSITION EXERCISES

### Comprehension Questions on the Model Composition

A.  1. Where was Lincoln born? When was he born?
    2. Where did his family move when he was a small boy?
    3. What did Lincoln have to do as a boy?
    4. How much formal education did Lincoln have?
    5. Where did Lincoln's family move when he was a young man?
    6. What did Lincoln study in his leisure time?
    7. What did he become?

8. What did he become famous for?
9. What did Lincoln believe?
10. What happened in 1860?
11. What did some of the Southern states do soon after his election?
12. What did this action bring on?
13. How long did the Civil War last?
14. When did Lincoln issue the Emancipation Proclamation?
15. What did this document proclaim?
16. Which amendment put an end to slavery in the United States?
17. Who won the Civil War?
18. Who shot Lincoln?
19. When did he die?
20. What did the world lose in his death?

## Vocabulary

*Opposites*

| | |
|---|---|
| formal education | informal education |
| justice | injustice |
| evil | good |
| slave state | free state |
| slavery | freedom |
| frontier | |
| oppose | |

## Word Forms

| *Verb* | *Adjective* | *Noun* | *Adverb* |
|---|---|---|---|
| oppose | opposite | opposition | |
| | | opposite | |
| proclaim | | proclamation | |
| create | creative | creation | creatively |
| | unjust | injustice | unjustly |
| debate | | debate | |
| secede | | secession | |

## Common Expressions

| | |
|---|---|
| to be born | to bring on |
| to be elected | to put an end to |
| to be shot | to come to an end |
| to earn a living | as of that date |
| to become famous for | in his leisure time |
| to set up | |

## Questions Using Common Expressions

B.
1. Where were you born? When were you born?
2. Who taught you to read and write?
3. What did your parents teach you to do?
4. Where did you live when you were a child?
5. What do you study in your leisure time?

6. Did you have to earn a living at an early age?
7. Who is the best-known person in your country?
8. When did the Second World War come to an end?
9. What did Thomas Edison become famous for?
10. How long does your English class last?
11. What do you do in your leisure time?

## STRUCTURE

**Irregular Verbs in the Model Composition**
teach — taught
have — had
become — became
study — studied (spelling)
withdraw — withdrew
bring — brought
bring on — brought on
set up — set up
put — put
come — came
shoot — shot
lose — lost

C. Fill in the blanks with the past tense of the verb in parentheses.
1. John Wilkes Booth _____ (shoot) President Lincoln.
2. The teacher _____ (put) the books on the desk.
3. I _____ (lose) my keys yesterday.
4. My father _____ (teach) me how to drive.
5. The cold weather _____ (bring on) an epidemic of influenza.
6. He _____ (withdraw) from the race when he broke his leg.
7. The countries _____ (set up) a conference to discuss nuclear disarmament.
8. We _____ (study) chemistry in high school.
9. The Second World War _____ (come) to an end in 1945.
10. She _____ (become) a dentist last year.
11. They _____ (bring) their lunch with them today.
12. The class _____ (have) an easy lesson last week.

*Must* **and** *have to*

*Must* — *have to* (show necessity): *had to* is the only past tense form for both *must* and *have to*.

| | |
|---|---|
| I *must* do it today. | I *had to* do it yesterday. |
| We *have to* do it today. | We *had to* do it yesterday. |
| | Lincoln *had to* work as a boy. |
| | He *had to* make a decision. |
| | They *had to* do their homework. |

Note the difference in meaning:

He *had* very little formal education. (past tense of *have*)
He *had to* earn a living. (past tense of *have to/must* — shows necessity)
What did you have for breakfast yesterday?
What did you have to do yesterday?

**D.** Working with a partner, change each sentence to the past tense. Remember to change the time to a past time, if necessary.

1. We have to do it right away.

_____

2. Everyone has to pay taxes in this country.

_____

3. We must call someone to fix the television set.

_____

4. They have to get up early every morning.

_____

5. I must meet my friend tonight.

_____

## Review of Active Voice and Passive Voice

| *Active Voice* | *Passive Voice* |
|---|---|
| 1                2                3 | 1                2                3 |
| *Performer* — *Action* — *Receiver of Action* | *Receiver of action* — *Action* — *Agent* |

| | |
|---|---|
| 1          2          3 | 1          2          3 |
| John Wilkes Booth shot Lincoln. | Lincoln was shot by John Wilkes Booth. |
| The people added the 13th Amendment to the Constitution. | *The 13th Amendment was added to the Constitution. |
| The plantation owners were to set the slaves free. | *The slaves were to be set free. |
| The people elected Lincoln President. | *Lincoln was elected President. |

*The agent is not necessary because it is understood in these sentences.

Note: The passive voice is used in the model composition because the receiver of the action was more important than the agent.

## Comparison of *well* + Past Participles Used as Adjectives

Lincoln was a *well-educated* man.
Lincoln was a *better-educated* man than his father. (comparative)
He was the *best-educated* man in his family. (superlative)
Lincoln was a *well-known* lawyer.
He was a *better-known* lawyer than his friend. (comparative)
He was the *best-known* lawyer in the state capital. (superlative)

The words *well, better, best* + *past participle* are usually hyphenated before a noun.

## ACTIVITIES

Listen to your teacher read the composition on John F. Kennedy. Then study the fact sheet below and write a composition following the fact sheet using the paragraph divisions indicated by the numbers I, II, III, and IV in Exercise E.

*John Fitzgerald Kennedy* (Fact Sheet)
I. Childhood and Early Years
  A. Born — Brookline, Massachusetts, in 1917.
  B. Second-oldest child. Family had nine children.
  C. Father — Joseph P. Kennedy. Prosperous businessman.
  D. Happy, lively family — supervised by maids and nurses — many sisters and brothers to play with.
II. Youth and Early Adulthood
  A. Father became Ambassador to England — Family went to live in London.
  B. Kennedy traveled a great deal — Became interested in international affairs.
  C. Graduated from Harvard during Second World War. Then enlisted in Navy.
  D. Served as Commander of a PT-boat in the Pacific. Discharged from Navy in 1945.
  E. Oldest brother, Joseph P. Kennedy, Jr., was supposed to enter politics. Joseph was killed in 1944 in the war. — Result: Kennedy decided to enter politics.
III. Maturity
  A. Congressman from Massachusetts 1946-1953. Senator from Massachusetts 1953-1960.
  B. Elected President in 1960. Age 43 — First Roman Catholic and youngest President.
  C. Inaugural Address — pledged his best efforts to help the people of the world help themselves. Told Americans "ask not what your country can do for you, ask what you can do for your country."

D. His program — "The New Frontier" — called for:
   a. Federal aid to education
   b. Medical care for the aged
   c. Peace Corps
   d. Alliance for Progress
   e. Major legislation to secure Civil Rights for Negroes
IV. End of Life
   A. Assassinated November 22, 1963, in Dallas, Texas.
   B. Fourth American President to die by an assassin's bullet. Great loss to the country and the world — had captured the hearts and minds of people everywhere in the world.

E. Write a composition of four paragraphs about the life of John F. Kennedy following the outline of facts. Begin each paragraph with the phrase or clause indicated:

*Paragraph I*
   John Fitzgerald Kennedy was born _____
   _____
   _____
   _____

*Paragraph II*
   When Kennedy was a young man, _____
   _____
   _____
   _____

*Paragraph III*
   From 1946 to 1953 _____
   _____
   _____
   _____

*Paragraph IV*
   On November 22, 1963, _____
   _____
   _____
   _____

# DICTATION / DICTO-COMP

*Martin Luther King, Jr.*

Martin Luther King, Jr., was born on January 15, 1929 in Atlanta, Georgia. Both his father and his maternal grandfather were Baptist ministers. King's paternal grandfather was a sharecropper for most of his life.

At the age of fifteen, King entered Morehouse College under a special program for gifted students. As an undergraduate he was interested in medicine and law, but in his senior year he decided to enter the ministry as his father had urged. After graduating from Morehouse, King spent the next three years studying at Crozer Theological Seminary in Pennsylvania where he received the bachelor of divinity degree. He was elected president of the student body and graduated with the highest academic average in his class. It was here that he first became acquainted with Mahatma Gandhi's philosophy of nonviolence. From Crozer he went on to Boston University where he was awarded a Ph.D. in 1955.

King began his civil rights crusade in 1955 when he led a boycott of buses in Montgomery, Alabama to protest discrimination against black passengers. At that time, black people in most Southern cities had to sit in the rear of public buses. The boycott was successful, and this convinced many people that civil rights could be won through nonviolent protest. He led civil rights demonstrations in many parts of the country, and as a result of these peaceful demonstrations, he received wide support from religious, labor, and civil rights organizations. King was arrested and jailed several times while protesting against injustice and discrimination. Partly as a result of his efforts, Congress passed the Civil Rights Act of 1964 which banned discrimination in voting, jobs, and public accommodations, and the Voting Rights Act of 1965 which protected the voting rights of Negroes. On August 28, 1963 in Washington, D.C., King gave a historic speech before hundreds of thousands of people in which he said, "I have a dream — a dream of the time when the evils of prejudice and segregation will vanish." Many people wept as they listened. In 1964, King received the Nobel Peace Prize for his efforts to bring peaceful change to America. He was the youngest person ever to receive this honor.

On April 4, 1968, King's life was cut short at the age of 39 when he was shot by an assassin in Memphis, Tennessee. His murder caused shock and grief throughout the world, and the President declared a national day of mourning to honor him. In his death, the country and the world lost a truly great man.

## COMPOSITION WRITING

**F.** Write a composition about a famous man or woman in your country. Follow the model composition and the outline below as much as possible.

*A Famous Man or Woman*
I. Childhood and Early Years
  A. Where was he/she born? When was he/she born?
  B. Were there any special influences or circumstances during his/her childhood?
  C. Where did he/she receive his/her early education?
II. Youth and Early Adulthood
  A. What special factors influenced this period?
  B. What further education or experiences did he/she have?
  C. What did he/she have to overcome in the way of difficulties?

III. Maturity
   A. What did he/she become?
   B. What did he/she believe in and fight for?
   C. What did he/she do for the people in your country?
IV. End of Life
   A. When and where did he/she die?
   B. Why and how do the people remember him/her today?
      1. Outstanding achievements
      2. Special holidays or celebrations

# Lesson 24

# Model Composition / Dialogue

This morning, as I was driving to work, a policeman saw me.

"Stop!" he said to me.

Then he asked me, "Where do you think you are going?"

"I am on my way to work," I answered.

"Is the place on fire?" he asked.

"My boss wants me to be on time," I said to him, "and he will get angry if I come late."

"You were driving too fast," the policeman said.

"I didn't realize it," I told him.

"Don't be in such a hurry," the policeman said. "Drive slowly and watch the traffic signals."

"I'll try to be more careful," I assured him.

Then I continued on my way.

---

### Quotations

Speech is the index of the mind.

PIETRO MANZOLI

Speech is the image of life.

DEMOCRITUS

There is a difference between speaking a lot and to the point.

ERASMUS

## COMPOSITION EXERCISES (PART 1)

### Questions on the Dialogue

A. Imagine that you are the driver in the dialogue, and answer in indirect speech wherever possible.

1. Where were you driving this morning?
2. Who saw you as you were driving to work?
3. What did he order you to do?
4. What did he then ask you?
5. What did you answer?
6. What did he ask you next?
7. What did you say to him in reply?
8. What did the policeman say about your driving?
9. What did you tell him?
10. What did the policeman then tell you?
11. What did you assure him?
12. What did you do then?

## MODEL COMPOSITION #2 / INDIRECT SPEECH

The following dialogue is the background for the model composition
*A Reported Conversation.*

*A Conversation*

Last night, John dreamed that he met Christopher Columbus and that
they had the following conversation:

JOHN: What are you doing now, Mr. Columbus?

COLUMBUS: I am still looking for a shorter route to India.

JOHN: What happened to that land you discovered in 1492?

COLUMBUS: I think it has become a country full of automobiles and television sets.

JOHN: What is the name of that country now?

COLUMBUS: I think it is called the United States of America.

JOHN: Did many of your men get seasick coming over to the New World?

COLUMBUS: I don't know what the word means.

JOHN: It isn't important. Tell me, do you think you will return to the
country you discovered?

COLUMBUS: I don't think so because the people speak English there now,
and I can't understand the language.

*A Reported Conversation*

Last night, John dreamed that he met Christopher Columbus and that
they had a conversation.

John asked Columbus what he was doing now, and Columbus answered
that he was still looking for a shorter route to India. Then John asked him
what had happened to the land he had discovered in 1492. Columbus replied
that he thought it had become a country full of automobiles and television
sets. Next, John asked him what the name of the country was now, and
Columbus said that he thought it was called the United States of America.
John then asked Columbus if any of his men had gotten seasick coming over
to the New World, and Columbus replied that he didn't know what the word
meant. John told him it wasn't important. Then John asked Columbus if he
thought he would return to the country he had discovered. Columbus replied that he didn't think so because the people spoke English there now, and
he couldn't understand the language.

## COMPOSITION EXERCISES (PART 2)

**Vocabulary and Common Expressions** (from both dialogues)

| | |
|---|---|
| to have a conversation | to look for someone or something |
| to be full of | to become full of |
| to be on one's way | to be on fire |
| to be on time | to be in a hurry |

to be careful
to get seasick
to get angry

to continue on one's way
I don't know what the word means
to realize something

## Questions on Vocabulary and Common Expressions

B.  1. With whom did you have a conversation this morning?
    2. What is this city full of?
    3. What were you looking for last night?
    4. Where did you stop on your way to school?
    5. Why are you in such a big hurry?
    6. When do you get seasick?
    7. Do you know what the word "parallel" means?
    8. Do you realize that you are getting older?
    9. When do you get angry?
    10. What time must you arrive in class to be on time?
    11. What was Columbus looking for in 1492?

# STRUCTURE

## Sequence of Tenses Rule

1. If the main clause is in a present tense, the noun clause may be in any tense that makes sense.

   He says he knows the answer.
   He says he is going tomorrow.
   He says he can do it.
   He says he will be here next week.
   *He says he went there yesterday.

2. If the main clause is in a past tense, then the noun clause is in a past tense.

   He said he knew the answer.
   He said he was going tomorrow.
   He said he could do it.
   He said he would be here next week.
   *He said he had gone there yesterday.

   *In indirect speech, when the verb in the quoted statement is in the past tense, the verb in the indirect statement (noun clause) is in the past perfect tense.

## Use of the Verbs *Say* and *Tell*

1. *Say:* When we give the exact words of the speaker, we always use *say*. *Say* cannot be used with an indirect object. It must be followed instead by a phrase with *to*.

   My mother *said*, "It is raining."
   Then she *said to me*, "Don't forget to take an umbrella."

2. *Tell:* When the exact words of a speaker are not given, you *say something*, but you *tell someone something.* The verb *tell* is often followed by an indirect object without *to.*

He *said* that the class was interesting.
He *told me* that the class was interesting.

## Direct and Indirect Speech

When we give the words of the speaker directly or exactly, it is direct speech. When we report the words of a speaker (or give them indirectly), it is indirect speech. Note that the Rule of Sequence of Tenses applies to indirect speech.

1. *Statements in Indirect Speech*

| *Direct Speech* | *Indirect Speech* |
|---|---|
| Mary said to me, "I don't know his name." | *Mary told me (that) she didn't know his name. |

*Tell* is usually used in all indirect sentences when the person to whom words were spoken is mentioned.

2. *Questions with Question Words*

An indirect question uses statement word order since the resulting sentence is no longer a question but a statement of fact. (It is sometimes called an included question.) Note the change in word order.

| *Direct Question* | *Indirect Question* |
|---|---|
| They asked, "How long will it take?" | They asked *how long it would take.* |
| He asked, "Where do you live?" | He asked *where I lived.* |
| John asked Mary, "When did you arrive?" | John asked Mary *when she had arrived.* |

3. *Questions without Question Words*

If a direct question does not begin with a question word, it is introduced by the word *if* or *whether* in the indirect question.

| *Direct* | *Indirect* |
|---|---|
| He asked me, "Do you speak French?" | He asked me $\left\{ \begin{matrix} if \\ whether \end{matrix} \right\}$ I spoke French. |
| The student asked the teacher, "Is tomorrow a holiday?" | The student asked the teacher $\left\{ \begin{matrix} if \\ whether \end{matrix} \right\}$ tomorrow was a holiday. |

4. *Imperative in Indirect Speech*

To express a request or a command in indirect speech we use the infinitive form of the verb.

| *Direct* | *Indirect* |
|---|---|
| The teacher said, "Take out your notebooks." | The teacher told us *to take out our notebooks.* |
| The guard said to John, "Don't smoke in this room." | The guard told John *not to smoke in this room.* |

5. *Summary of Direct and Indirect Speech*

In Indirect Speech, if the main clause is in a past tense, the noun clause must be in a past tense.

*Direct*                                    *Indirect*

a. *Statement*

I said, "Mary is a good student."

I said (that) Mary was a good student.

He said to me, "I am busy."

He told me that he was busy.

b. *Question*

He asked, "Where does John work?"

He asked where John worked.

He asked, "What time did you get up?"

He asked what time I had gotten up.

"Do you like your class?" he asked Mary.

He asked Mary $\begin{Bmatrix} if \\ whether \end{Bmatrix}$ she liked her class.

He asked me, "Did you enjoy the program?"

He asked me $\begin{Bmatrix} if \\ whether \end{Bmatrix}$ I had enjoyed the program.

c. *Imperative*

She said to me, "Come back later."

She told me to come back later.

He said to us, "Don't sit there!"

He told us not to sit there.

**C.** Change the following sentences from direct speech to indirect speech.

1. The conductor said, "The train will leave in five minutes."
2. The man asked me, "What country do you come from?"
3. My neighbor said, "I will be glad to help you."
4. The teacher asked us, "Where did John go?"
5. "Do you like this food?" the hostess asked me.
6. "Can you tell me where the university is?" I asked the policeman.
7. "I have studied English for a year," John informed me.
8. The policeman said to us, "Don't cross against the lights."
9. My friend said, "Soccer is the most popular game in Brazil."
10. Then he added, "Most Brazilians don't understand baseball."
11. The doctor said to me, "Eat a balanced diet."
12. Mrs. Smith said, "Please try to come early."

**D.** Read the following story and then give the actual words spoken (direct speech). In the last sentence, be sure to change to indirect speech.

*An Italian in the United States*

An Italian was once traveling in the United States. He knew some English but his vocabulary was not large.

Once, while he was eating in a small country inn, he wanted to order some eggs, but he couldn't think of the word for eggs. Suddenly, through the window, he saw a rooster walking in the yard. He immediately asked the waiter what the bird was called in English. The waiter told him that it was called a rooster. Then the Italian asked what the rooster's wife was called. The waiter answered that she was called a hen. The Italian then asked what the hen's children were called. The waiter told him that they were chickens. The Italian then asked what the chickens were called before they were born. The waiter told him they were called eggs.

"That's the word!" said the Italian. "Please bring me two sunny-side up, some toast, and a cup of coffee."

## ACTIVITIES

**E.** Working in pairs, write a dialogue between a reporter and E.Z., a visitor from another planet. The reporter will ask five questions which E.Z. will answer. When you have finished writing the dialogue, act it out in front of the class. The other students will then repeat it in reported speech.

## DICTATION / DICTO-COMP

*The Hare and the Tortoise*

The hares always boasted about their speed. One of them made fun of a tortoise because he was so slow. For a while the tortoise stayed silent, but one day he tired of the teasing.

"I may be slow," he said to the hare, "but if we ever have a race I will win."

"Ridiculous!" said the hare.

"Is it?" said the tortoise. "We shall see right now. Are you ready?"

They started immediately, and the hare quickly outran the tortoise.

He was, in fact, so far ahead that he treated the whole thing as a joke and lay down on the grass. "I'll take a little nap," he said to himself, "and when I wake up I'll finish the race far ahead of the tortoise."

However, the hare overslept. When he arrived at the finish line, the tortoise, who had plodded steadily along, was there ahead of him.

*Moral:* The race is not always to the swift. Slow and steady is bound to win.

AESOP

## COMPOSITION WRITING

**F.** First, read the reported speech paragraph about John and Columbus. Then, read the dialogue between the policeman and the driver. Now, write this dialogue in a paragraph of a reported (indirect) speech as though you were relating the incident to someone.

# Model Composition / The American Family

The most common type of family in the United States is the nuclear family. The nuclear family is typically made up of two generations — parents and their still-dependent children. The typical family is middle-class, and there is usually some kind of equality between the husband and wife. Each family lives in its own separate residence, and it is not usual to share a house with one's grandparents or in-laws. American families are very mobile and are continually changing jobs and moving to other neighborhoods. It is estimated that an average American family moves about once every five years. The care of children in an American family is exclusively the responsibility of their parents, and children are taught to be independent at an early age. Adult children usually leave their parents' house and set up their own households even though they are not married.

The American family today is undergoing real change. For example, American families have fewer children today and some choose to have none. In addition, more mothers are working due to a combination of economic reasons and the changing social climate. Divorce is quite common, and one of the most disturbing changes is that millions of children are being brought up by one parent, usually the mother. Nevertheless, most divorced people remarry, and many of these remarriages include a child from a former marriage. Therefore, there are many new patterns of family life emerging in the United States.

---

**Quotations**

The security and elevation of the family and of family life are the prime objects of civilization, and the ultimate ends of all industry.

CHARLES W. ELIOT

The family is one of nature's masterpieces.

GEORGE SANTAYANA

All happy families resemble one another, every unhappy family is unhappy in its own way.

TOLSTOY

## COMPOSITION EXERCISES

**Comprehension Questions on the Model Composition**

A.  1. What is the most common type of family in the United States?
    2. What is the nuclear family?
    3. How many generations usually live in a typical American family home?

4. What is the usual relationship between husband and wife?
5. How often does an average American family move?
6. Who is exclusively responsible for the care of children?
7. What are children taught to be at an early age?
8. What do adult children usually do? (Why do you think they do this?)
9. Are American families today larger or smaller than before?
10. Why are more mothers working today?
11. What is one of the most disturbing changes in family life?
12. What happens to most divorced people?
13. How is this changing the pattern of American family life?

## Vocabulary and Common Expressions

| | | |
|---|---|---|
| nuclear family | mobile | social climate |
| to be made up of | exclusively | to bring up |
| divorce | to undergo | to emerge |

## Questions on Vocabulary and Common Expressions

**B.**
1. Do you think the nuclear family pattern is a good model in today's world? Why?
2. How does one get a divorce in your country?
3. Who helped your parents bring you up?
4. Should household chores be exclusively a wife's duties?
5. How mobile are families in your country?
6. Where does a butterfly emerge from?
7. What kind of students is this class made up of?
8. Is the social climate changing in your country? (For example, is it acceptable for women to work?)
9. What kind of tests do astronauts have to undergo before they can go into space?

# STRUCTURE

## Linking Words

Linking Words (or Transition Words) are connecting words that help the reader understand how one sentence is related to another. Some of the uses of linking words are as follows:

1. To give examples or illustrations — *for example, for instance*

    The American family is undergoing real change. *For example*, American families have fewer children and some choose to have none.

    John is a very impolite person. *For instance*, he is always interrupting a conversation.

2. To show a contrast between the details in two sentences — *nevertheless, in spite of this, however, but, on the other hand*

    Divorce is quite common. *Nevertheless*, most divorced people remarry.

    Many children would like to take care of their elderly parents. *However*, it is not always possible.

    New York is a fun city. *In spite of this*, I wouldn't want to live there.

3. To show additions to details — *moreover, in addition*

Many families cannot take care of their parents because the majority of American women work. *Moreover*, houses and apartments are smaller than they used to be.

Mary is a full-time student. *In addition*, she works part-time.

4. To make clear the connection between two sentences where the first sentence states a cause and the second sentence states the result or effect — *consequently, in this way, therefore, so, for this reason, because of this, as a result*

The majority of American women are currently working, *so* it is not always possible to take care of an elderly relative.

The majority of women are currently working. *Consequently*, it is not always possible to take care of an elderly relative.

The majority of American women are currently working. 
{ *For this reason, Because of this, Therefore, As a result,* } 
it is not always possible to take care of an elderly relative.

**C.** Link the following pairs of sentences with connecting words from (1), (2), (3), or (4) above.

1. I had a very bad cold. I went to school.
2. The snow made the road very slippery. There were many accidents.
3. My neighbor's radio was very loud last night. I couldn't sleep.
4. Mary is in love with John. John is in love with Ellen.
5. The astronauts took a television camera to the moon. The whole world could see the first walk on the moon.
6. Jack plays the piano well. He also sings well.

**D.** Add a second sentence to the following first sentence using each of the listed linking words.

*Man has made tremendous scientific progress in this century.*

For example, _____

For instance, _____

In spite of this, _____

Nevertheless, _____

However, _____

On the other hand, _____

Therefore, _____

As a result, _____

For this reason, _____

Because of this, _____

## DICTATION / DICTO-COMP

*The Elderly*

Americans over 65 are probably the fastest growing age group in the country. By the year 2030, according to the U.S. Census Bureau, nearly one-quarter of the United States population will be over 65. The major reasons for this graying of America are recent medical advances that have conquered many diseases that used to be fatal, so that more people are living longer.

As a result of major social and economic changes in the United States, families, the traditional support system in other countries, are not in a position to take care of their elderly relatives. The majority of American women are currently working. Consequently, the traditional role of daughter or daughter-in-law as care-giver has become obsolete. Moreover, houses and apartments are often smaller than they used to be. Also, increased mobility has separated and spread families over thousands of miles. Despite a willingness, children may be unable to take care of a parent. More often than not, however, it is the older people who do not want to move in with their children.

## COMPOSITION WRITING

E.  Following the model composition and the outline below, write a composition about the typical family in your country. Make use of transition words.

> *The _____ Family*
> I. The Family Today
>    A. Size and composition of typical family
>    B. Mobility of family
>    C. Relationship between husband and wife in family
>    D. Children
>        1. Position of children in family structure
>        2. Responsibility for raising the children
>        3. Adult children — position and responsibilities
>    E. Position and duties of elderly relatives
> II. Changes in Patterns of Family Life
>    A. Causes for the change
>    B. Effects of change on family life

# Model Composition / Time Capsule

If I were asked to select five items to represent American life today that would be placed in a 3' × 3' × 3' time capsule not to be opened until the year 5000, I would choose the following items. The first item would be a pair of jogging shoes. This would represent the American people's craze for physical fitness at present. Next, I would include a picture of a hamburger and of a roadside MacDonald's or Burger King. Fast food chains are proliferating all over the country, and the pictures would represent an American food habit. The third item would be a computer. We are living in a computer age today, and it is predicted that every child will soon become familiar with the computer in school, and that every business and most homes will soon have one as well. The fourth item would be the book, *How to Live to Be 100 — or More*, by George Burns. This is advertised as "the ultimate diet, sex, and exercise book" and would be an example of the kind of book that always appears on America's best-seller lists. The last item would be a videotape of a few soap operas. On this one could see the clothes of today, the homes of today, and some of the problems Americans face in their social life. When they open the capsule in the year 5000, I wonder what the people of the future will think of us.

---

**Quotations**

Inevitably, the culture within which we live shapes and limits our imagination . . . .
MARGARET MEAD

Culture is roughly anything we do and the monkeys don't.
LORD RAGLAN

We have changed our environment more quickly than we know how to change ourselves.
WALTER LIPPMANN

## COMPOSITION EXERCISES

**Comprehension Questions on the Model Composition**

A. Imagine you are the writer of the model composition, and answer in complete sentences.
  1. How large is the time capsule?
  2. What would the articles represent?

3. What is the first item you would select? Why?
4. What is the next item? Why would you choose this item?
5. Why would you choose a computer as one of the items?
6. What kind of book would you select? What would this be an example of?
7. Why would you choose a videotape of a soap opera?
8. When will the time capsule be opened?

## Vocabulary and Common Expressions

| | |
|---|---|
| jogging | to proliferate |
| craze | to become familiar with |
| physical fitness | soap opera |
| fast food chains | |

## Questions on Vocabulary and Common Expressions

B.
1. How popular is jogging in your country? Do you jog?
2. What is the latest fashion craze in your country?
3. What do you do to maintain your physical fitness?
4. Do they have fast food chains in your country? What kind of fast food chains do they have?
5. What kind of government bureaus are proliferating in your country?
6. Have you become familiar with the customs of this country? What customs have you become familiar with?
7. Are soap operas popular in your country? Which ones? Who watches them?

## STRUCTURE

### Use of the Conditional in the Present Unreal

A present unreal condition usually suggests a situation which is unreal or contrary to fact.

In expressing a present unreal condition we use a past tense, or a modal auxiliary (would, should, might, could) and the Simple Verb, in the *if* clause. In the main clause we use the modal auxiliary *would, should, might,* or *could* and the main verb.

| *If Clause* | *Main Clause* |
|---|---|
| 1. If I had a million, | I could take a trip around the world. |
| *2. If today were Sunday, | we wouldn't be here. |
| 3. If I could spend my life in Hawaii, | I would be very happy. |
| 4. If we invited him, | he might come. |
| *5. If I were you, | I would have nothing to do with that girl. |

*In the *if clause* in the present unreal, with the verb *to be,* we use the form *were* for 1st, 2nd, and 3rd persons, singular and plural.

**C.** Complete the following sentences using the present unreal conditional.

    1. If Mary had the time, _____

    2. If you were the only woman/man in the world, _____

    _____

    3. If I could live my life again, _____

    4. If I were the head of my country, _____

    5. If everyone made love instead of war, _____

**D.** Complete the following sentences:

    1. She would pass the examination if _____

    2. Tom wouldn't be so fat if _____

    3. I couldn't work twelve hours a day if _____

    4. The airplane wouldn't land if _____

    5. Animals would be like human beings if _____

**E.** Working with a partner, fill in the blanks with the correct form of the verb.

My birthday _____ (fall) on February 23, in the middle of winter. On that day I generally _____ (go) out to dinner and the theater with a few friends, and I usually _____ (receive) some thoughtful presents from them.

If I could spend my birthday as I liked, I _____ (invite) about ten friends to a birthday party at my house in the evening. I _____ (serve) champagne, and we _____ (toast) each other on the occasion. We _____ (talk) about happy things, dance, play amusing games, and entertain each other. At about eleven o'clock I _____ (serve) a light supper. Then I _____ (cut) the birthday cake, and I _____ (give) each of my guests a piece while they sang "Happy Birthday." After supper, I _____ (play) the guitar for them, and we _____ (sing) together. When it _____ (be) time to leave, I _____ (give) each of my friends a gift of something I knew he wanted, either a book, a record, or tickets to a play. In this way I _____ (try) to express how much pleasure his friendship gave me.

## ACTIVITIES

**F.** Working in groups, list five more items representing American life that you would put in a time capsule 3' × 3' × 3'. Explain why you would choose these items.

## DICTATION / DICTO-COMP

In 1938 a time capsule was placed in the ground at the site of the 1939 New York World's Fair. The contents of the capsule were chosen to indicate what life was like in the nineteen-thirties. Dozens of specialists participated in the choice. Among the items placed in the capsule was a large amount of microfilmed reading matter, including a variety of newspapers and magazines, a World Almanac, and a newsreel of the news events of that period. The capsule also contained many articles in common use, including a telephone, a can-opener, a woman's hat, a wristwatch, a package of cigarettes, a slide rule, and a lump of coal. There were also samples of textiles, plastics, and a variety of seeds.

In 1965 another time capsule was placed in the ground near the same site for the opening of the second New York World's Fair. Both time capsules are to be opened in the year 6939, five thousand years after the first fair closed.

## COMPOSITION WRITING

**G.** As a specialist in the culture of your country, you have been asked to choose five items to be placed in a 3' × 3' × 3' time capsule. The capsule won't be opened until the year 5000 and will give the people of the future an idea of life in your country today.

Follow the model composition, and complete the outline below to write your own one-paragraph composition on:

*A Time Capsule*
A. Opening sentence
B. Items chosen and reasons why
C. Concluding sentence

# Model Composition / American Humor

American humor is difficult to define because Americans are such a diverse people. In the early days, when the country was largely agricultural, America's humor derived from stories about people in rural areas. Then, as the country developed and became more urban and industrialized, there were many jokes contrasting the sophistication of the city dweller and the naiveté of the country folk. Here is an example of one such story.

An artist driving through a rural area saw a quaint rustic* with a picturesque mountain in the background.

"I'll give you twenty dollars if you let me paint you," he said.

The mountaineer kept chewing his tobacco in silence as he thought it over.

"You wouldn't have to do anything for the money," the artist added, trying to persuade him.

"I'm not thinking about the money," said the rustic, "I was just wondering how I'd get the paint off when you're finished."

Today, American humor has been adapted and restyled to reflect the new conditions of present day life. The following is an example.

As the airplane took off from O'Hare Airport, a metallic voice came over the loudspeaker: "Ladies and gentlemen, Vista Airlines would like to welcome you to the first transatlantic flight that is being controlled completely by computer. The possibility of human error has been eliminated because there is no pilot and no crew aboard. All of your needs will be taken care of by the very latest technology. Just relax and enjoy your flight. Every contingency has been prepared for, and nothing can possibly go wrong . . . go wrong . . . go wrong."

A good appreciation of humor is healthy both for a country and an individual. People laugh at different things, but if you can laugh at yourself, then you have a truly mature sense of humor.

*rustic — an unsophisticated rural person

**Quotations**

Everything is funny as long as it is happening to somebody else.
WILL ROGERS

Joking and humor are pleasant, and often of extreme utility.
CICERO

Humor is gravity concealed behind the jest.
JOHAN WEISS

## COMPOSITION EXERCISES

### Comprehension Questions on the Model Composition

**A.**
1. Why is American humor difficult to define?
2. Where did American humor derive from in the early days?
3. How did the country develop?
4. What kind of jokes became popular as the country developed?
5. Where was an artist driving one day?
6. What did he see?
7. What would the mountaineer have to do for the money?
8. What has happened to American humor today?
9. In the second joke, what kind of voice came over the loudspeaker?
10. Who was speaking?

### Vocabulary and Common Expressions

to reflect
to derive from
sophisticated vs. naive (adjectives)
sophistication vs. naiveté (nouns)
urban vs. rural
contingency
to think something over

to persuade someone to do
   something
immigrant vs. emigrant
to adapt
to restyle
to eliminate
to be prepared for

### Questions on Vocabulary and Common Expressions

**B.**
1. Do you believe a person's clothes reflect his or her character? Explain.
2. What languages does English derive from?
3. Do you consider yourself sophisticated or naive in money matters?
4. Where do most people in the large urban areas in your country come from?
5. How long did you think it over before you decided to come here?
6. Who persuaded you to take this course?
7. What customs did you find it difficult to adapt to in this country?
8. How did you restyle your mode of living?
9. Do you have a contingency fund to cover illness?
10. How do you eliminate grammatical errors?
11. Were you prepared for the last test?
12. What countries are large numbers of immigrants to this country coming from today?

## STRUCTURE

### Clauses

A principal clause (independent clause) is a group of words with a subject and a predicate. It is a sentence in itself.

The tall man is my uncle.

A subordinate clause (dependent clause) is a group of words with a subject and a predicate that cannot stand alone as a sentence. A dependent clause (subordinate) depends on a word or a group of words in a main clause to give it meaning.

The tall man [*who is talking to Millie*] (dependent clause) is my uncle.

There are three kinds of subordinate clauses — adjective clauses, noun clauses, and adverbial clauses. The kind of work a subordinate clause does in a sentence determines what kind of clause it is.

## Adjective Clauses

1. An adjective clause acts like an adjective in a sentence. It tells you something about a noun (or a pronoun). It usually follows the noun it modifies.

   I would like to welcome you to this flight *which is controlled by computer.*
   Many immigrants *who came in the early part of this century* didn't know the language.
   I met the man *whose son won the prize.*

2. Adjective clauses usually begin with the relative pronouns *who, whose, whom, which, that.* Relative pronouns connect or "relate" the adjective clause to the noun it modifies. A relative pronoun can be the subject or the object of a verb, or it can be the object of a preposition in a clause.

   I met the boy *who comes from France.* (*Who* is subject of the verb *come.*)
   The boy *whom I met* comes from France. (*Whom* is object of the verb *met.*)
   The boy *to whom I spoke* comes from France. (*Whom* is object of the preposition *to.*)

   When a relative pronoun is the object of a verb, the relative pronoun may be omitted.

   The boy *I met* comes from France.

   When a relative pronoun is the object of a preposition it may be omitted. Note that the preposition is shifted to the end of the clauses.

   The boy *I spoke to* comes from France.

   Adjective clauses can also begin with relative adverbs like *where, when, why.* The relative adverb connects or "relates" the adjective clause to the noun it modifies.

   Rural jokes were popular in the days *when the country was agricultural.*

**C.** Complete the following sentences using adjective clauses.

   1. This is the house where _____ .

   2. The lawyer whom _____ lives in San Diego.

   3. The class which _____ starts at 9:00 A.M.

   4. The woman whose _____

      speaks French fluently.

   5. Thomas Edison is the man who _____ .

**D.** Combine the following sentences. Use sentence (b) as the adjective clause.

    1. a. The dog bit the man.
       b. The dog belongs to Mr. Smith.
    2. a. I admire that ballet dancer.
       b. The ballet dancer studied in Moscow.
    3. a. The dog bit the man.
       b. The man owns that white house.
    4. a. The movie was interesting.
       b. I saw the movie last night.

**E.** Working with a partner, write five sentences using adjective clauses. Use different relative pronouns. Underline the adjective clause and mark the noun it modifies.

## Noun Clauses

A noun clause acts like a noun in a sentence. It is a subordinate clause that can be used as the subject or object of a sentence, the object of a preposition, or the predicate complement. Noun clauses can begin with *who, whose, what, which, when, why, where, how, if, whether,* or *that.*

  1. *Noun clause used as object of verb*

    The teacher asked me *what plans I had for the future.*
    The artist asked the rustic *if he could paint him.*
    The rustic was wondering *how he would get the paint off.*
    I learned *that people don't laugh at the same jokes.*
    He showed me *what he had bought.*
    He told me *where the library was.*

  2. *Noun clause as subject of a sentence*

    *How you feel* is important to me.
    *What you do after school hours* is your own concern.

  3. *Noun clause as object of a preposition*

    I am interested in *how your health is.*
    They talked about *where they were going on vacation.*

  4. *Noun clause as a predicate complement*

    The morning hours are *when I work best.*
    This is *where he lives.*

**F.** Complete the following sentences using noun clauses.

    1. I believe _____

_____

    2. I asked the policeman _____

_____

    3. I don't know _____

_____

4. The doctor said _____

_____

5. The teacher told us _____

_____

**G.** Working with a partner, write five sentences containing a noun clause. (Use noun clauses as object of verb, subject of verb, predicate complement, and object of a preposition.) Mark the noun clause and identify its function in the sentence.

## Adverbial Clauses

Adverbial clauses act like adverbs. Adverbial clauses are subordinate clauses that modify a verb, an adjective, or an adverb in a sentence.

1. *Adverbial clause modifying a verb*

a. An adverbial clause can tell you *when, how, for what reason,* or *for what purpose* an action is done.

I learned to drive *before I finished high school.*
He lived in a small town *when he was young.*
She learned to speak French *because most of her friends spoke French.*
*When I graduated from high school,* I started attending night college.*
He got up early *so that he could jog before work.*

*When the adverbial clause precedes the main clause, it is set off by a comma.

b. When an adverbial clause begins with *if* or *unless,* it tells you under what conditions the verb in the main clause occurs.

I usually watch television at night *unless I have a test the next day.*
You will catch a cold *if you don't wear a warm coat.*

c. When an adverbial clause begins with *although* or *even though,* it tells you an opposing or contrasting statement about the verb.

John likes his job *although he works hard.*
She speaks English well *even though she was born abroad.*

2. *Adverbial clause modifying an adjective or adverb*

a. Used in comparing adjectives and adverbs

Tom is more intelligent *than I am.*
Tom works harder *than I do.*

b. Adverbial clauses of comparison are sometimes incomplete. They are called elliptical clauses.

Tom is more intelligent *than I.*
Tom works harder *than I.*

3. Adverbial clauses can start with words like *when, wherever, while, after, before, if, unless, as if, although, because, so that,* and *since.* These words that introduce adverbial clauses are called subordinating conjunctions. This means that they connect the sentence parts by joining the adverbial clause in a dependent (or subordinating) manner to the main clause.

My wife was happy. I came home late. (2 independent or main clauses.)

My wife was happy $\begin{cases} \textit{if} \\ \textit{when} \\ \textit{unless} \\ \textit{because} \\ \textit{although} \end{cases}$ I came home late.

Note the difference in meaning of the subordinating conjunctions.

**H.** Complete the following sentences using adverbial clauses so that they will answer the question words in parentheses. Use different subordinating conjunctions.

1. I was late _____

   _____ (For what reason?)

2. He will speak English well _____

   _____ (When?)

3. I started this course _____

   _____ (When?)

4. He came to school _____

   _____ (Under what conditions? — use *unless*)

5. I didn't carry an umbrella _____

   _____ (In spite of what? — use *although* or *even though*)

6. She needs the money _____

   _____ (For what purpose?)

7. I park my car _____

   _____ (Where?)

8. I practice my English _____

   _____ (When?)

**I.** Working with a partner, write five sentences containing an adverbial clause. Use adverbial clauses of reason, opposition, condition, comparison, and purpose. Mark the adverbial clause and identify its function in the sentence.

## DICTATION / DICTO-COMP

For Americans, the anecdote* has always been a popular form of humor.

*The Uglier Man*

Lincoln was, naturally enough, very surprised one day when a man with a very disagreeable look drew a revolver and thrust the gun into his face. In such circumstances Lincoln at once decided that any attempt at debate or argument was a waste of time and words.

"What seems to be the matter?" inquired Lincoln with all the calmness and self-possession he could manage.

"Well," replied the stranger, who did not appear at all excited, "some years ago I swore that if I ever came across an uglier man than myself I'd shoot him on the spot."

A feeling of relief evidently took possession of Lincoln at this answer, and the expression upon his face lost all suggestion of anxiety.

"Shoot me," he said to the stranger, "because if I am an uglier man than you, I don't want to live."

*anecdote — a short interesting or amusing story about a real person or event

## COMPOSITION WRITING

**J.** Read the model composition, and then write a composition following the outline about humor in your country.

*Humor in* _____
   A. Type of humor popular in your country
   B. Reason for this type of humor
   C. Example of joke or anecdote
   D. How this type of humor reflects conditions in your country

# Model Composition / How Would You Change the World?

I asked my friends what they would do to change the world if they could. My mother said with a laugh: "Sew up everybody's mouth! Then people would be judged by what they do and not by what they say." My brother said: "Improve communications. Let people meet and talk directly with each other instead of going by stereotypes on TV."

My social worker friend said: "First, give food to all." But my spiritual friend said: "Even if everyone's material needs were met, people would not be fully satisfied until they had a deeper direction inside. Meditation is the key." Then my cook friend combined the two ideas and said, "Teach nutrition in the schools. How can people have the proper thoughts if they do not eat the right foods? If they would eat more vegetables, they would become more enlightened for vegetables are a higher consciousness food."

I asked my diplomat friend and he said in a solemn voice: "Establish peace." My secretary friends said: "We must learn to get along with our own families, friends, and co-workers before we can expect peace in the world. And we should start by giving both men and women of all ages and colors an equal chance to fulfill their destinies." My old friend the scholar too recommended that we all be a little kinder to each other. However, my psychologist suggested that we do just the opposite and release our pent-up hostilities.

My accountant friend advised the rich to give to the poor and to stop caring more about money than about people. But my psychic friend, having studied the stars, said: "It will take some great natural disaster, such as a fire or a flood, to shock people into really caring about each other."

My writer friend wrote to me, saying: "Deep in our hearts we all know the answer; to change the world, we must change ourselves. If everyone swept his own doorstep, the street would be clean." Along the same lines, my friend the philosopher told me that the answer lies in each of us doing at all moments what he thinks is right and not what he thinks is "expedient, or comfortable, or profitable, or popular, or safe, or impressive." Yet my friend the photographer offered more concrete **suggestions**: "Install flushless toilets, ban cars, bring back the bicycle!" said she.

To add to my confusion, my yogi friend said he didn't think the world needed any improving as the Garden of Eden is a place in the mind.

So finally I turned to God and asked if it could all somehow be stated more simply. And He said: "Love."

© Jyoti Carty
United Nations Secretariat News, April 1977

There are no grammar or vocabulary exercises in this composition. This is a free final composition to give you confidence in your writing ability. Before you write this composition, review the grammar in Compositions 25, 26, and 27.

Composition #25: Transition Words

Composition #26: Present Unreal Conditional

Composition #27: Clauses (Adjective, Noun, Adverbial)

Read the model composition and then write a composition on "How I Would Change the World." Give four ways in which you would change the world and explain what the changes would do. Plan your composition and outline it before you start to write. Good luck!

# A SHORT HANDBOOK

# Symbol Chart for Correction of Compositions

The compositions you write will be marked for corrections with the symbols listed below. The errors will be underlined (or otherwise marked) in the text. The specific type of error will be indicated in the left margin of your paper. Therefore, be sure to leave a wide margin on the left side of your paper.

## SYMBOLS IN THE TEXT

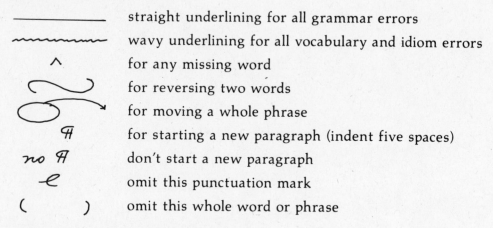

| | |
|---|---|
| ——————— | straight underlining for all grammar errors |
| ∿∿∿∿∿∿ | wavy underlining for all vocabulary and idiom errors |
| ∧ | for any missing word |
| ∽ | for reversing two words |
| ⟲→ | for moving a whole phrase |
| ¶ | for starting a new paragraph (indent five spaces) |
| no ¶ | don't start a new paragraph |
| ℓ | omit this punctuation mark |
| ( ) | omit this whole word or phrase |

## SYMBOLS IN THE LEFT MARGIN

| | |
|---|---|
| sp. | spelling errors |
| punc. | punctuation errors |
| cap. | capitalization errors |
| # | errors in number (singular/plural) |
| det. | determiner errors (articles — a, an, the) |
| prep. | preposition errors |
| wd. | wrong vocabulary item or word form |
| t. | error in verb tense |
| agr. | error in subject-verb agreement |
| ref. | error in reference |
| ? | something I can't understand |

# Irregular Verbs in English

| Present | Past | Past Participle |
|---|---|---|
| arise | arose | arisen |
| | | |
| be (am, is, are) | was, were | been |
| bear | bore | born, borne |
| beat | beat | beat, beaten |
| begin | began | begun |
| bend | bent | bent |
| bet | bet | bet |
| bind | bound | bound |
| bite | bit | bit, bitten |
| bleed | bled | bled |
| blow | blew | blown |
| break | broke | broken |
| bring | brought | brought |
| build | built | built |
| burst | burst | burst |
| buy | bought | bought |
| | | |
| catch | caught | caught |
| choose | chose | chosen |
| come | came | come |
| cost | cost | cost |
| cut | cut | cut |
| | | |
| deal | dealt | dealt |
| dig | dug | dug |
| do | did | done |
| draw | drew | drawn |
| drink | drank | drunk |
| drive | drove | driven |
| | | |
| eat | ate | eaten |
| | | |
| fall | fell | fallen |
| feed | fed | fed |
| feel | felt | felt |
| fight | fought | fought |
| find | found | found |
| flee | fled | fled |
| fly | flew | flown |
| forbid | forbade | forbidden |
| forget | forgot | forgotten |
| forgive | forgave | forgiven |
| freeze | froze | frozen |
| | | |
| get | got | got, gotten |
| give | gave | given |
| go | went | gone |
| grind | ground | ground |
| grow | grew | grown |

| Present | Past | Past Participle |
|---|---|---|
| hang | hung, hanged | hung, hanged |
| have, has | had | had |
| hear | heard | heard |
| hide | hid | hidden, hid |
| hit | hit | hit |
| hold | held | held |
| hurt | hurt | hurt |
| keep | kept | kept |
| know | knew | known |
| lay | laid | laid |
| lead | led | led |
| leave | left | left |
| lend | lent | lent |
| let | let | let |
| lie | lay | lain |
| light | lit, lighted | lit, lighted |
| lose | lost | lost |
| make | made | made |
| mean | meant | meant |
| meet | met | met |
| mistake | mistook | mistaken |
| pay | paid | paid |
| put | put | put |
| quit | quit | quit |
| read | read | read |
| ride | rode | ridden |
| ring | rang | rung |
| rise | rose | risen |
| run | ran | run |
| say | said | said |
| see | saw | seen |
| seek | sought | sought |
| sell | sold | sold |
| send | sent | sent |
| set | set | set |
| sew | sewed | sewn, sewed |
| shake | shook | shaken |
| shine | shone | shone |
| shoot | shot | shot |
| show | showed | shown, showed |
| shut | shut | shut |
| sing | sang | sung |
| sink | sank | sunk |
| sit | sat | sat |
| sleep | slept | slept |

| Present | Past | Past Participle |
|---|---|---|
| speak | spoke | spoken |
| spend | spent | spent |
| spread | spread | spread |
| stand | stood | stood |
| steal | stole | stolen |
| stick | stuck | stuck |
| sting | stung | stung |
| swear | swore | sworn |
| sweep | swept | swept |
| swim | swam | swum |
| swing | swung | swung |
| | | |
| take | took | taken |
| teach | taught | taught |
| tear | tore | torn |
| tell | told | told |
| think | thought | thought |
| throw | threw | thrown |
| | | |
| understand | understood | understood |
| undertake | undertook | undertaken |
| uphold | upheld | upheld |
| upset | upset | upset |
| | | |
| wake | woke, waked | waked |
| wear | wore | worn |
| weep | wept | wept |
| win | won | won |
| wind | wound | wound |
| withdraw | withdrew | withdrawn |
| wring | wrung | wrung |
| write | wrote | written |

# Conversion Tables

## CONVERTING METRIC TO U.S. MEASUREMENTS

| Multiply: | by: | to find: |
|---|---|---|
| *Length* | | |
| millimeters (mm) | .039 | inches (in) |
| meters (m) | 3.28 | feet (ft) |
| meters | 1.09 | yards (yd) |
| kilometers (km) | .62 | miles (mi) |
| *Area* | | |
| hectares (ha) | 2.47 | acres |
| *Capacity* | | |
| liters (L) | 1.06 | quarts (qt) |
| liters | .26 | gallons (gal) |
| liters | 2.11 | pints (pt) |
| *Weight* | | |
| grams (g) | .04 | ounces (oz) |
| kilograms (kg) | 2.20 | pounds (lb) |
| metric tons (MT) | .98 | tons (t) |
| *Power* | | |
| kilowatts (kw) | 1.34 | horsepower (hp) |
| *Temperature* | | |
| degrees Celsius | 9/5 (then add 32) | degrees Fahrenheit |

## CONVERTING U.S. TO METRIC MEASUREMENTS

| Multiply: | by: | to find: |
|---|---|---|
| *Length* | | |
| inches (in) | 25.40 | millimeters (mm) |
| feet (ft) | .30 | meters (m) |
| yards (yd) | .91 | meters |
| miles (mi) | 1.61 | kilometers (km) |
| *Area* | | |
| acres | .40 | hectares (ha) |
| *Capacity* | | |
| pints (pt) | .47 | liters (L) |
| quarts (qt) | .95 | liters |
| gallons (gal) | 3.79 | liters |

| Multiply: | by: | to find: |
|---|---|---|
| *Weight* | | |
| ounces (oz) | 28.35 | grams (g) |
| pounds (lb) | .45 | kilograms (kg) |
| tons (t) | 1.11 | metric tons (MT) |
| *Power* | | |
| horsepower (hp) | .75 | kilowatts |
| *Temperature* | | |
| degrees Fahrenheit | 5/9 (after subtracting 32) | degrees Celsius |

## SIMPLE PRESENT TENSE

**Verb** *to be*

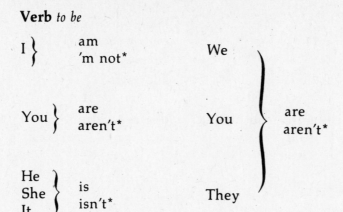

*Note:
*I'm not* is the negative contraction for *I am not*
*isn't* is the negative contraction for *is not*
*aren't* is the negative contraction for *are not*

**Other Verbs**

| I You | work don't work* | We | |
| --- | --- | --- | --- |
| | | You | work don't work* |
| He She It | works doesn't work* | They | |

*Note:
*don't* is the negative contraction for *do not*.
*doesn't* is the negative contraction for *does not*.

### Use of the Simple Present Tense

The simple present tense is used:

1. to make a statement of fact
   Bananas grow on trees.
   Michiko comes from Japan.
   Washington, D.C. is the capital of the United States.
2. to express customs and habitual actions
   The English drink a lot of tea.
   My son watches television every night.
   She often works late.

3. to express opinions
   Richard is a good cook.
   This milk tastes sour.
   He doesn't like spinach.

# PRESENT CONTINUOUS TENSE

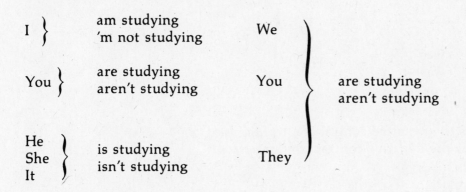

I { am studying / 'm not studying

We }

You { are studying / aren't studying

You { are studying / aren't studying

He / She / It } is studying / isn't studying

They }

## Use of the Present Continuous Tense

The present continuous tense is used:

1. to express an action that is happening at the moment of speaking or writing
   I am sitting in the library and writing you this letter.
   Many children are playing in the park.

2. to express an activity or situation that is happening over a given period of time
   She is studying French this semester.
   I am reading a book about Lincoln this week.
   They are living in Chicago at present.

*Note:* There are some verbs that don't usually take a continuous form. These verbs express mental states or conditions or some form of perception. Use them in the present simple tense.

*Verbs Not Used in a Continuous Form*

| Mental State | | | Condition | Perception |
|---|---|---|---|---|
| believe | like | remember | belong | feel |
| think | love | forget | own | smell |
| (opinion) | need | | have | taste |
| know | prefer | | (possess) | hear |
| seem | want | | owe | see |
| understand | wish | | cost | |
| | | | mean | |
| | | | resemble | |

## SIMPLE PAST TENSE

**Verb** *to be*

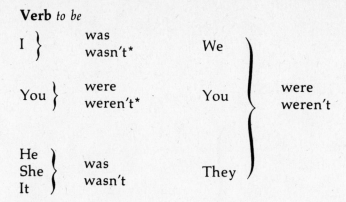

I } was / wasn't*    We }

You } were / weren't*    You } were / weren't

He / She / It } was / wasn't    They }

*Note:
*wasn't* is the negative contraction for *was not*
*weren't* is the negative contraction for *were not*

**Other Verbs**

I / You / He / She / It } walked / didn't walk*

We / You / They } walked / didn't walk

*Note:
*didn't* is the negative contraction for *did not*

### Use of the Simple Past

The simple past tense is used:

1. to express an action or an event in the past that is completed
   My parents lived in Arizona for ten years. (They no longer live there.)
   Joan didn't come to school yesterday.
   Neil Armstrong was the first man to walk on the moon.

## PAST CONTINUOUS TENSE

I } was talking / wasn't talking    We }

You } were talking / weren't talking    You } were talking / weren't talking

He / She / It } was talking / wasn't talking    They }

## Use of the Past Continuous Tense

The past continuous tense is used:

1. to express an action that was happening at a specific moment in the past
   He was doing his homework at eight o'clock last night.
   They were eating dinner when the telephone rang.
2. to express two actions that were happening at the same time in the past
   The students were talking to each other while the teacher was writing on the blackboard.

# PRESENT PERFECT TENSE

I }
have talked
haven't talked*

We

You }
have talked
haven't talked

You

}
have talked
haven't talked

He
She
It }
has talked
hasn't talked*

They

*Note:
*haven't* is the negative contraction for *have not*
*hasn't* is the negative contraction for *has not*

## Use of the Present Perfect Tense

The present perfect tense is used:

1. to express an action that started in the past and is still continuing
   They have been here for two hours. (They are still here.)
   She has lived in Europe since 1982. (She still lives there.)
   We have finished fifteen lessons so far. (We haven't finished the book yet.)
2. to indicate an action that happened at an unspecified time in the past. When the time is given, the simple past is used.

| | | |
|---|---|---|
| We have already eaten lunch | *but* | We ate lunch at noon. |
| She has gone to the museum three times. | *but* | She went to the museum in July, August, and September. |
| I have seen that movie. | *but* | I saw that movie last week. |

3. to express an action that was completed in the immediate or recent past
    They have finished their work at last.
    He has finally gotten a promotion.
    We have just bought a new car.
    She has recently started a new job.

## PRESENT PERFECT CONTINUOUS

| I, You | have been talking / haven't been talking | We, You, They | have been talking / haven't been talking |
| He, She, It | has been talking / hasn't been talking | | |

### Use of the Present Perfect Continuous

The present perfect continuous is used:

1. to express the continuous nature of an activity that started in the past and is still continuing at present. It is usually used with *since* and *for*.
    They have been studying in the library since three o'clock.
    She has been working here for five years.

*Note:* The present perfect and the present perfect continuous are often interchangeable.
    Verbs not used in the other continuous tenses are not used in this tense either.

## PAST PERFECT TENSE

| I, You, He, She, It | had talked / hadn't talked* | We, You, They | had talked / hadn't talked |

*Note:
*hadn't* is the negative contraction for *had not*

### Use of the Past Perfect Tense

The past perfect tense is used:

1. to express an action or an event in the past that happened before another action in the past
    He went to bed after he had finished his work.
    By two o'clock, Dr. Miller had performed three operations.
    Kennedy had been president for three years when he was killed.

174

# FUTURE TENSE

I
You
He    } will talk
She      won't talk
It

We
You    } will talk
They     won't talk

*Note:
*won't* is the negative contraction for *will not*

## Use of the Future Tense

The future tense is used:

1. to express an action or an event that will happen after the present time
   We will play tennis tomorrow.
   She will be twenty years old next year.
2. to express a promise of action
   I will meet you after class.

## Other Ways of Expressing Future Time

Future time in English can also be expressed in different ways.

*Be going to + simple verb*

1. to express a planned or intended action

   We are going to have a party tomorrow.
   They are going to visit their parents next week.

*Note:* The use of *will* and *be going to* to express future time are often inter-changeable.

*Simple Present and Present Continuous Tenses*

1. for verbs that express arriving, departing, starting, and finishing

   The train leaves at two o'clock this afternoon.
   My class starts at nine o'clock tomorrow morning.
   The plane is arriving in ten minutes.
   My parents are returning from Europe next week.

*Note:* A future time word is necessary when the present simple or present continuous tense is used to express future time.

# Paragraphs and Compositions

In this section you are going to learn how to write paragraphs and compositions in the English language. Each lesson in the first part of the book will help you improve your writing ability through practice in different styles. First, however, it is necessary to understand the meaning and organization of a paragraph and composition in the English language.

## PARAGRAPHS

A paragraph is a group of sentences that talks about only one idea. We call this one idea *the topic* of the paragraph.

A paragraph is a convenient way of presenting the writer's thoughts in an organized form.

### Characteristics of a Paragraph

1. A paragraph develops just one topic.
2. Every sentence in a paragraph says something about the topic of the paragraph.
3. The first line of every paragraph is indented. This means that the first line begins a little further to the right than the other lines in the paragraph.

———————————————————— · ————
—————————————— · ————————————————
—— · ————————————————————————

4. There is no set rule for the length of a paragraph. It can consist of one sentence or of many sentences. It should be long enough to make its topic clear to the reader. As a general rule, your paragraphs for the lessons in this book will be about five sentences in length.

### The Topic Sentence

Many paragraphs are built around *a topic sentence.* A topic sentence states in general terms the main thought of the paragraph. The other sentences in the paragraph explain, discuss, or illustrate the idea stated in the topic sentence. The topic sentence is usually the first sentence in a paragraph. Sometimes, however, it appears in the middle or at the end of the paragraph.

A paragraph doesn't need to have a topic sentence. If a paragraph doesn't have a topic sentence, all the sentences in the paragraph still express one central idea.

### Essentials of a Good Paragraph

1. A good paragraph is *adequately developed.* This means that you must tell enough about the central idea to make it clear to the reader.
2. A good paragraph has *unity.* This means that all the sentences in the paragraph talk about the central idea (or topic).

3. A good paragraph has *coherence*. This means that the sentences in the paragraph are arranged in a logical order. Coherence also means that all the sentences are linked together so that the reader can follow the thoughts as they move from one sentence to another.

## Organization of a Good Paragraph

There are different ways of arranging the details of a paragraph.

1. *Using chronological (or time) order* — If you are telling a story or giving directions, the order will usually be chronological. This means the order in which the details happened, were done, or should be done.

   *How to Scramble Eggs* (Lesson 8)
   *A Typical Day* (Lesson 9)
   *Abraham Lincoln* (Lesson 23)

2. *Using space order* — If you are writing a description of something you see, you can arrange the sentences starting at the details that are near you and then moving to those further away, or from top to bottom or right to left. This is called space order.

   *Description of Classroom* (Lesson 2)

3. *Using the order of general or topic statement* — If you use a topic sentence that makes a general statement, you can then follow it up by adding details, giving examples, or explaining the topic statement.

   *Bad Habits* (Lesson 13)
   *The American Family* (Lesson 25)
   *American Humor* (Lesson 27)

4. *Using comparison and contrast order* — This order is used to describe two persons or things. You can present all the details about the first and then follow with details about the other. Or, you can take up the differences and similarities one at a time and show how the two are alike or different.

   *A Comparison of Two Cities* (Lesson 6)
   *Two Friends* (Lesson 19)

5. *Using problem-solution order* — If you are using a problem-solution order in writing your composition, you will first tell what the problem is and, where applicable, give the causes of the problem. Then you will suggest solutions to the problem and explain why you chose these solutions.

   *Time Capsule* (Lesson 26)
   *How Would You Change the World?* (Lesson 28)
   *An Unusual Dream* (length) (Lesson 15)
   *The Classroom* or *A letter to a Friend* (different word order) (Lessons 2 and 3)

## Sentence Variety

A paragraph composed of sentences that are all of the same structure or the same length can be very dull. In order to make your paragraph more interesting and alive, it is a good idea to use sentence variety. One way to do this is to vary the length of your sentences. Another way is to vary the word order of the sentences.

### Summary for Writing Good Paragraphs

1. Indent the first line of a paragraph.
2. A paragraph should be long enough so that it can be clearly understood by the reader.
3. The paragraph should contain only one central idea. This can be stated in a topic sentence.
4. Every sentence in the paragraph should relate to the central idea.
5. Try to use a variety of sentences.
6. The paragraph should have adequate development, unity, and coherence.

# COMPOSITIONS

A composition is a piece of writing made up of one or more paragraphs. A composition has a subject (or theme) that can be broken down into a number of topics. Each topic in a composition should have its own paragraph.

A new paragraph generally follows a change in thought from one part of a topic to another, or from the general idea to a specific case. A new paragraph is a signal for these changes of thought. For example, if you were writing a composition on "The United States," this would be the subject of the composition. This could then be broken down into two paragraphs with the following topics:

I. Physical Characteristics
II. The People

If you were writing a composition on the "Life of Abraham Lincoln," this would be the theme. This could then be broken down chronologically into the following four paragraphs.

I. Childhood Years
II. Youth and Early Adulthood
III. Maturity
IV. End of Life

Each paragraph in a composition is a part of the subject of the whole composition. The wording of each paragraph depends on the paragraph that comes before it and the paragraph that follows it.

### Essentials of a Good Composition

1. A good composition limits the content of the composition to one subject (or theme).
2. A good composition presents and develops the subject matter in an orderly manner.
3. A good composition sticks to the subject of the composition.
4. A good composition shows continuity from one paragraph to the next in the same way that sentences do within a paragraph.

## Organization of the Composition

Many compositions can be arranged basically as follows:

1. *Introduction* — The introduction usually tells the reader what the composition is about (generalization).
2. *Body* — The body of a composition tells the story or explains the facts.
3. *Conclusion* — The conclusion ends the composition. It is usually a short summary of your ideas or the last details of a story (generalization).

These three divisions do not tell exactly where each topic idea goes. In order to write a well-planned composition, it is necessary to decide where each topic should be. One way to do this is to organize the details of a composition through the use of *an outline*.

An outline is a detailed plan of your composition.

## Purpose of an Outline

1. An outline tells you what to write.
2. An outline sets out the order in which your thoughts should be written.
3. An outline tells you how to paragraph your composition.
4. An outline helps you stick to the subject of the composition from the beginning to the end.

## Preparing an Outline

When you write an outline you list very briefly and in the proper order the ideas you wish to include in your composition. Then you write the composition following the outline. If your outline is well-arranged, your composition will be well-arranged.

For paragraph divisions use Roman numerals I, II, III, etc. For subdividing a paragraph, use the capital letters A, B, C, etc., indenting them evenly. If you want to subdivide still more, use the Arabic numerals 1, 2, 3, etc., and indent again. For even more subdivision, indent again and use the lower case letters a, b, c, etc. Place a period after each number or letter.

Outline form for topic or sentence outline:

I. _____
  A. _____
    1. _____
      a. _____
      b. _____
    2. _____
  B. _____
    1. _____
    2. _____
      a. _____
      b. _____
    3. _____
II. _____
  A. _____
  B. _____
  C. _____

## Two different kinds of outlines

1. *The Topic Outline* — This is the most common form of outline. The topics and sub-topics are noted in brief phrases or single words and are numbered and lettered consistently. No punctuation is needed after the topics in a topic outline.

    *An Important Object*
    I. A Childhood Favorite Object
        A. Description of object
        B. How you got it
        C. What you did with it
        D. Meaning of object to you
    II. Present-day Memories
        A. How you feel about the object today
        B. What happened to the object

2. *The Sentence Outline* — In this outline each head or sub-head is a complete sentence. Each sentence in a sentence outline needs a period or a question mark.

    *A Typical Day in My Life*
    I. Morning
        A. At what time do you get up in the morning?
        B. What do you do before you leave for school or work?
        C. What time do you leave for school or work?
    II. Getting to School or Work and the Afternoon
        A. How do you get to school or work?
        B. What do you do or see on your way?
        C. How long does it take you to get to school or work?
        D. What are your hours at school or work?
        E. What do you do afterwards?
        F. What time do you leave for home?
    III. Evening
        A. What do you do when you get home?
        B. What time do you have dinner?
        C. What do you do after dinner?
        D. At what time do you go to bed?
        E. How long do you sleep?

## The Different Types of Compositions

*Description*

The descriptive composition describes something or someone. It tells how a person or a thing appealed to the senses, that is, how it looked, sounded, smelled, tasted, or felt.

There are two different kinds of description:

1. *Description to give information* — When writing a description to give information, be sure to include enough details for clarity and to arrange your details in an orderly way so that it is easy for the reader to understand.

   *The Classroom* (Lesson 2)
   *A Letter to a Friend* (Lesson 3)

2. *Description of animals or persons* — When writing a description of people, carefully select the outstanding features or traits that distinguish them from other people. Also, describe what the people do as well as how they act.

   *My Classmate* (Lesson 11)
   *Two Friends* (Lesson 19)

## Narration

A composition in narrative style tells a story. It tells what a person or thing did during a particular period of time. The span of time can be of short duration or it can cover a long period. In narrative writing, events are described in the order of their happening. This type of composition follows a chronological (or time) order with one action following another as it happened in the original experience.

When writing a narrative composition, be sure that you create interest through movement of actions in the story and that you include enough details for clearness.

   *My First Day in the United States* (Lesson 16)
   *First Flight* (Lesson 22)
   *Abraham Lincoln* (Lesson 23)

## Exposition

All expository writing deals with facts and ideas. This expository type of writing gives the reader information.

The subject matter of an expository composition may:

1. *Present factual information* — When writing an exposition to present factual information, be sure your facts are correct and clearly expressed. Also make certain that the facts are arranged in a logical order and that there is a single central theme.

   *The United States* (Lesson 4)
   *The American Family* (Lesson 25)

2. *Explain a process* — When writing an exposition to explain something, (a) divide your explanation into steps, (b) arrange the steps in the order in which they should be performed, (c) include all the necessary information, and (d) use words that give the exact information.

   *How to Scramble Eggs* (Lesson 8)

## Linking Sentences

In order for the reader to be able to move from one sentence to another easily, it is necessary that the sentences be tied together in some way. Sometimes, the best way to link sentences is to use connecting words that show how one sentence is related to another.

For example, we said that in narrative writing it is important to show time relationship between sentences. Adverbial linking expressions like the following help you do this:

| | |
|---|---|
| First . . . | As soon as I arrived home . . . |
| Then . . . | Before eating dinner . . . |
| After that . . . | After dinner . . . |
| Finally . . . | The next morning . . . |

When writing descriptive paragraphs, it is very important to use direct linking expressions. The reader must not only see the details but also know how they are related to one another. The following linking expressions help show how the details are related:

| | |
|---|---|
| To the right . . . | At the top . . . |
| In the center . . . | Under the windows . . . |
| In the corner . . . | As you turn left . . . |
| Directly in front of . . . | On the opposite side . . . |

When writing an expository paragraph explaining how to make or do something, linking expressions like the following help the reader follow the steps of the process smoothly:

| | |
|---|---|
| First . . . | After adding the lemon . . . |
| Next . . . | Before turning on the oven . . . |
| After that . . . | |
| Then . . . | |

When writing a paragraph of comparison or contrast, you can emphasize the contrast with linking words like the following:

| | |
|---|---|
| On the one hand . . . | Yesterday . . . |
| On the other hand . . . | Today . . . |
| In spite of . . . | However . . . |
| But . . . | Nevertheless . . . |

When you want to make clear the connection between two sentences, where the first sentence states a cause and the second states a result or effect, you can tie the sentences together with one of the following linking words or expressions:

| | |
|---|---|
| Therefore . . . | Consequently . . . |
| So . . . | As a result . . . |
| For this reason . . . | Because of this . . . |

# *Letters*

Much of the business in the world today is carried on by mail. Everyone has occasion to write letters at some time, either business or personal. Your letters represent you on paper. In order to make the best possible impression, it is important to know the forms and conventions (wordings) one must follow in writing letters. In this chapter you will find models of common business and personal letters that will help you learn how to write letters.

## BUSINESS LETTERS

There are many different kinds of business letters. Among the most useful ones to know are the letter of request, the letter of complaint and adjustment, and the order letter.

The following is a list of things to remember when writing a business letter:

1. A business letter should always be typed, if possible. (If you must write it, use a pen and dark ink. Never write a business letter in pencil.)
2. Use plain white paper (stationery).
3. Be sure your letter is neat and attractive.
4. Write on only one side of the paper. If you need more paper, use a second sheet.
5. State all the necessary information clearly and briefly without omitting important details.
6. State the purpose of the letter at the beginning. Be sure that the rest of your letter is related to that purpose.
7. Be courteous and friendly.
8. Your envelope should match your stationery.
9. Be sure your return address is in the upper left hand corner of the envelope.
10. Proofread each letter before you mail it.
11. Make a copy of the business letter for your own file.

### Parts of a Business Letter

There are six parts of a business letter. They are: the heading, the inside address, the salutation, the body of the letter, the complimentary closing, and the signature.

## Form of a Business Letter

*Heading:*
_____
_____
_____

*Inside*
*Address:*
_____
_____
_____

*Salutation:* _____

*Body (Message):*
_____
_____
_____
_____

*Complimentary Closing:* _____

*Signature:* _____

---

205 West End Avenue
New York, NY 10023
November 8, 19 _____

American Language Institute
New York University
1 Washington Square North
New York, NY 10003

Gentlemen:

Would you kindly send me the spring catalogue of English courses offered at the American Language Institute.

I have recently arrived in this country from Korea, and I would like to take some courses to improve my English.

Very truly yours,
Peter Yoon

---

### Heading

The heading of a business letter consists of the complete address of the sender and the date of the letter. The heading is usually written with no punctuation at the end of each line.

### Inside Address

When you write to a company, put the complete name and address of the company above the salutation.

When you write to an individual, make sure to include his or her full name and title as well as his or her address.

*Business Salutations*

| *When writing to a:* | *Use the following salutation:* |
| --- | --- |
| Company | Gentlemen: |
| Man | Dear Mr. Smith: |
| | Dear Sir: |
| Single Woman | Dear Miss Jones: |
| Married Woman | Dear Mrs. Brown: |
| | Dear Madam: |
| Woman, but you don't know whether she is single, married, or divorced | Dear Ms. Brown: |

Place a colon (:) after the salutation.

*The Body of the Letter*

The body of the letter is the main part of the message and states the purpose of writing the letter.

*Complimentary Closing*

In business letters there are a number of different closings you may use:

| *Very formal* | Respectfully yours, | Yours respectfully, |
| --- | --- | --- |
| *Formal* | Yours truly, | Very truly yours, |
| *Informal* | Sincerely yours, | Yours sincerely, |
| *Friendly* | Cordially yours, | Cordially, |
| | | Sincerely, |

Place a comma after the complimentary closing.

*Signature*

The signature is the name of the person who wrote or dictated the letter. It should always be written by hand. When signing a business letter, always write your full name.

| *Man* | John W. Smith |
| --- | --- |
| *Single woman* | (Miss) Mary L. Brown |
| *Married woman* | Helen Smith |
| | (Mrs. John W. Smith) |

If you have an official position, you should write your title after or under your signature:

Martin F. Stone, Director     Helen W. Smith
Stanley L. Brown     Assistant Professor
Executive Secretary

## Addressing an Envelope

Write your own name and address in the upper left hand corner of the envelope. If the mail carrier cannot find the person to whom the letter is sent, the letter will be returned to you.

Write the complete name and address of the firm near the center of the envelope. When writing to a person, include his full name and title and the name of the company and the address of the company for which he works.

Be sure to include the ZIP Code number both in your own address and in the address to which the letter is sent.

```
┌─────────────────────────────────────────────────────────────┐
│                                                             │
│   Mrs. Gerald Chen                        ┌───────────────┐ │
│   13 Main Street                          │               │ │
│   Grand Rapids, MI 49503                  │     Stamp     │ │
│                                           │               │ │
│                                           └───────────────┘ │
│                                                             │
│                                                             │
│                                                             │
│                Magic Quartz Corp.                           │
│                408 Communipaw Avenue                        │
│                Jersey City, NJ 07304                        │
│                                                             │
│                                                             │
│                                                             │
└─────────────────────────────────────────────────────────────┘
```

## TYPES OF BUSINESS LETTERS

### Letters of Request

**A.** Requests for booklets, catalogues, samples, etc.

This is one of the most commonly used types of business letters. You may want to send for a catalogue, a sample of merchandise, or a booklet. You must state in your letter exactly what you want. If you want a booklet or a catalogue, give the exact title. If you saw something advertised in a newspaper, in addition to an exact description of the item, give the date and the name of the newspaper where you saw the item.

Letters of request for pamphlets or other items offered publicly need only identify the request and give adequate information for its delivery.

*Samples*
*(Letter to American Language Institute asking for a catalogue)*

205 West End Avenue
New York, NY 10023
November 8, 19 _____

American Language Institute
New York University
1 Washington Square North
New York, NY 10003
Gentlemen:

Would you kindly send me the spring catalogue of English courses offered at the American Language Institute.

I have recently arrived in this country from Korea, and I would like to take some courses to improve my English.

Very truly yours,
Peter Yoon

*(Letter to Success Story Magazine asking for booklet)*

2773 E. 47th Street,
Tulsa, OK 74131
December 8, 19 _____

Success Story Magazine
Two Center Plaza
Boston, MA 02109

Gentlemen:

 Would you kindly send me your booklet "How to Become a Millionaire" as advertised in the December issue of "Success Story Magazine."

 I am enclosing 50¢ in coin to cover the cost of handling and mailing.

Very truly yours,
Jack Powell

*Exercise:*

1. Write to a company asking for a travel folder, a sample advertised in a magazine, or a booklet.
2. Write to a university asking for a catalogue.

**B.** Requests for information

A letter requesting information should be courteous. The best way to be courteous is to use words like "please" and "I would appreciate." Another way is to be as brief as possible and to state what you want as clearly as possible.

*Sample*
*(Letter to Foreign Student Admissions Office asking for information and application form)*

325 East 70th Street
New York, NY 10021
January 10, 1984

Office of Undergraduate Foreign Admissions
New York University
25 West 4th Street
P.O. Box 9090 Cooper Station
New York, NY 10276

Gentlemen:

 Please send me a catalogue and an application form for admission to the College of Arts and Sciences, New York University. I have finished twelve years of school in Greece and I have my transcripts with me. I arrived in this country two months ago and I would like to enter the freshman class in September 1984. My major field of interest is economics.

 I would appreciate any additional information you could send me about the cost of tuition and of living on campus. I also would like to know about any scholarships or other assistance available to foreign students.

 Thank you very much.

Sincerely yours,
Eleni Papadopoulos

(*Note:* Application for admission to a college in the United States must be made from 2–8 months in advance of the desired enrollment date.)

*Exercise:*
1. Write to a university and ask for a catalogue and an application form for admission to a college.
2. Write to a Record Club (Book Club, etc.) and ask for a catalogue explaining how to become a member of that club.

## Letters of Complaint and Adjustment

Letters of complaint and adjustment are sent when some error has occurred in the course of a business transaction. The customer should assume that the mistake was not committed intentionally, and that the company will be glad to adjust the matter once it understands the circumstances. Therefore, a first letter of complaint should be calm, courteous, and tactful.

A letter of complaint and adjustment should include the following information:
1. Begin your letter by stating the circumstances of the transaction.
2. Give all the necessary details explaining simply and courteously what is wrong.
3. Explain the adjustment you want made.

*Sample*
*(Letter of complaint and adjustment)*

70 Park Terrace West
San Jose, CA 95128
November 21, 19 _____

Macy's Order Dept.
Box 1280
San Francisco, CA 94132
Gentlemen:

On November 14th I ordered by phone one pair of women's black, cashmere-lined Italian leather gloves, size 6½, at $32.00 a pair. When they were delivered yesterday, I found that you had sent size 8 instead of the size requested.

Would you please send the correct order as soon as possible and arrange to pick up the package you sent by mistake.

Very truly yours,
Gladys L. Rowen
(Mrs. Frank Rowen)

*Exercise:*
1. Pretend that something has gone wrong with the toaster (radio, record player, etc.) you have just bought. Write a letter of complaint and adjustment to the company telling them about it. Follow the suggestions for writing letters of adjustment given above.
2. The book club which you belong to has sent you a bill for two books that you did not order and have not received. Write a letter explaining in detail why you are returning the bill unpaid.

## Order Letters

Your order letters must be very clear and complete. The letter should describe the articles wanted and include all the necessary details such as item number, size, color, style, quantity wanted, and price. If necessary, include the shipping instructions. Also mention how you want to pay for the merchandise. If you saw the article advertised in a newspaper or a magazine, be sure to mention which publication and the date of the advertisement.

*Sample*
*(Order Letter)*

520 9th Avenue
Belmar, NJ 07719
November 21, 19 _____

Wallachs
32-36 47th Avenue
Long Island City, NY 11101
Gentlemen:

Please send me the following article, advertised in the November 20th New York Times:

| | | |
|---|---|---|
| 1 | #3L, Men's Racquet Club Shetland wool crewneck sweater from the Shetland Isles of Scotland, Size Large, yellow color | $45.00 |
| | Handling Charge | 1.95 |
| | Total | $46.95 |

I am enclosing a check in the amount of $46.95 to cover the cost of the sweater plus the handling charge.

Very truly yours,
Joseph Argan

*Exercise:*

1. Write a letter ordering merchandise, repairs, or tickets for a concert or show.
2. Write a letter ordering something you saw advertised in a newspaper or magazine advertisement.

## PERSONAL OR SOCIAL LETTERS

Personal letters (also called friendly notes or social letters) are short letters used to extend, accept, or refuse an invitation and to express thanks, get-well wishes, or congratulations.

When you write such letters, be sure to sound sincere and natural.

The following is a list of things to remember when writing a personal letter:

1. Be sure that your letter is neat and attractive.
2. Use a white or light colored sheet of paper.
3. Write neatly in pen and ink. Don't use a pencil.
4. Discuss things which will interest the person to whom you are writing.

5. Write in a friendly and natural style.
6. Your envelope should match your stationery.
7. Be sure to include your address and date in the letter.
8. Sign your name clearly, using your full name if you are not writing to close friends.
9. Be sure your return address is in the upper left hand corner of the envelope.

## Parts of a Personal Letter

There are five parts of a personal letter. They are: the heading, the salutation, the body of the letter, the complimentary closing, and the signature.

## Form of a Social Letter

*Heading (Date)* _____
_____
_____

*Salutation:* _____
*Body (Message):* _____
_____
_____
_____
_____

*Closing:* _____
*Signature:* _____

---

                                            110 Wilson Road
                                            Bedford, MA 01730

Dear Mr. Howard,                     February 21, 19 _____

   My husband and I would be very happy if you could come to dinner on Friday night, March third, at seven o'clock in the evening. We are having a small informal party afterwards. We hope you can join us.

                                      Sincerely yours,
                                      Janet Roberts
                                      (Mrs. William Roberts)

---

*Heading*

The heading of a social letter should include your complete address and the date of the letter. The heading is usually written with no punctuation at the end of each line.

   Write the name of the month of the year in full.

*Salutation for a Social Letter*

| When writing to a: | Use the following salutation: |
|---|---|
| Friend | Dear Betty,<br>Dear Harold, |
| Single Woman | Dear Miss Seymour, |
| Married Woman | Dear Mrs. Jones, |
| Woman, but you don't know whether she is single, married, or divorced | Dear Ms. Taylor, |
| Man (single or married) | Dear Mr. Edwards, |

Place a comma after the salutation.

*Note:* Instead of "Dear Mr. Edwards" you can say "My dear Mr. Edwards" when you write to someone whom you do not know very well.

*The Body of the Letter*

The body of the letter is the main part of the message and states the purpose of writing the letter.

*Closing a Social Letter*

In a friendly letter you may use the following endings:

| *Formal* | Sincerely yours,<br>Very sincerely, | Sincerely,<br>Very sincerely yours, |
|---|---|---|
| *For people you don't know well or haven't seen for some time* | As always,<br>As ever, | |
| *Very friendly closings* | Affectionately,<br>Fondly, | Love, |

*Signature in a Social Letter*

If you are writing to a close friend or relative who knows you and your address, sign your first name only:

    Tom          Roberta          Jerry

If you are writing to a friend who doesn't know you too well, or if your first name will not identify you clearly, write your full name.

    John W. Smith        Jennie I. Jones

If a woman is married, she should always write her own first name in her signature. She may add her married name under her name, if necessary.

    Janet Roberts
    (Mrs. William Roberts)

*Addressing an Envelope*

Write your own name and address in the upper left hand corner of the envelope. If the mail carrier cannot find the person to whom the letter is addressed, the letter will be returned to you.

Write the complete name and address of your friend near the center of the envelope.

Be sure to include the ZIP Code number both in your own address and in the address to which the letter is sent.

```
┌────────────────────────────────────────────────────────────┐
│                                                            │
│  Mrs. William Roberts                        ┌───────────┐ │
│  110 Wilson Road                             │           │ │
│  Bedford, MA 01730                           │   Stamp   │ │
│                                              │           │ │
│                                              └───────────┘ │
│                                                            │
│                                                            │
│              Mr. Richard Howard                            │
│              17 Shade Street                               │
│              Lexington, MA 02173                           │
│                                                            │
│                                                            │
│                                                            │
└────────────────────────────────────────────────────────────┘
```

## TYPES OF PERSONAL LETTERS

### Informal Invitations

A letter of invitation should sound sincere and cordial. Be definite in giving the time and place of the affair and indicate whether it is going to be formal or informal.

*Sample*
*(Letter of Invitation)*

110 Wilson Road
Bedford, MA 01730
February 21, 19 _____

Dear Mr. Howard,

My husband and I would be very happy if you could come to dinner on Friday night, March third, at seven o'clock. We are having a small informal party afterwards. We do hope you can join us.

Sincerely yours,
(Mrs.) Janet Roberts

*Exercise:*

Write a letter to a friend inviting him or her to a concert (a football game, a dance, or a picnic).

### Note of Acceptance

Acknowledge invitations promptly and express your appreciation for an invitation sincerely. To avoid confusion, repeat the time, place, and date of the affair you have been invited to.

*Sample*
*(Note of Acceptance)*

17 Shade Street
Lexington, MA 02173
February 24, 19 _____

Dear Mrs. Roberts,
  I will be very glad to dine with you and your husband on Friday, March third, at seven o'clock and to attend the party afterwards. It was very nice of you to ask me.

Yours sincerely,
Richard Howard

*Exercise*
Write a letter of acceptance to someone who has invited you to a dinner (concert, football game, picnic).

## Note of Refusal

A letter of regret is written when you cannot accept an invitation to an affair. Be sure to acknowledge the invitation promptly. Express pleasure that you were invited and tell why you cannot accept the invitation.

*Sample*
*(Letter of Refusal)*

17 Shade Street
Lexington, MA 02173
February 24, 19 _____

Dear Mrs. Roberts,
  I am very sorry that I will not be able to dine with you and your husband on Friday, the third of March. Unfortunately, I expect to be in Chicago on that day.
  Thank you for asking me, and I hope you will give me the opportunity to say "yes" some other time.

Sincerely yours,
Richard Howard

*Exercise*
Write a letter expressing your regret for your inability to accept an invitation to a concert (picnic, dinner, etc.)

## Bread-and-Butter Letter

A bread-and-butter letter is a letter of thanks written for entertainment overnight or longer. You should mention something noteworthy about the event in your letter. It doesn't have to be a long letter, but it should be written naturally and sincerely. It should express the appreciation of the writer for the hospitality that he has received.

*Sample*
*(Bread-and-Butter Letter)*

11 Waverly Street
Columbus, OH 43210
October 20, 19 _____

Dear Mrs. Johnson,

It is a pleasure to write this letter because it gives me an opportunity to tell you how much I enjoyed your hospitality last weekend. It was my first visit to an American family and, at first, I was very anxious about my limited English and my knowledge of the customs. Then I saw you and your children waiting for me at the station with warm smiles of welcome on your faces. I immediately knew that everything was going to be all right. You and your wonderful family put me at ease right away.

There are many happy memories of the weekend that I will keep with me forever. How can I mention them all? Above all, I will remember that you made me feel "right at home." There were so many new and different things for me to see and do. I particularly enjoyed driving through the countryside with Mr. Johnson and you and seeing the changing colors of the leaves on the trees. I liked playing baseball and *Monopoly* with your sons, Jimmy and Joey. They were very patient with me and full of fun. Tell them I will teach them how to play soccer next time. I also had a good time at the Community Square Dance on Saturday night. It was my first square dance, and I cannot forget how friendly and kind everyone was.

I am back at school again now and I am very happy because I now know a real American family and it is one of the nicest families I have ever met. Because my English is still not very good, I cannot express my feelings better. I can only say "Thank you" and hope that someday you will visit my country and I can return your hospitality.

Sincerely yours,
Carlos Gomez

*Exercise:*

Write a bread-and-butter letter to someone at whose house you have stayed a few days. Follow the model letter and the following outline but try to be as natural as possible.

*A Bread-and-Butter Letter*
 I. Arrival at Host's Home
   A. Topic sentence — Thank the host or hostess for the hospitality.
   B. The Journey
     1. How you felt during the trip
     2. Anything that happened on the way
   C. Safe Arrival
     1. How you felt when you got there
     2. People waiting for you
 II. Hospitality
   A. General statement of the good time you had there.
   B. Particulars of anything you particularly enjoyed and why
     1. What you enjoyed doing and seeing
     2. Any particular food or custom that was new to you

III. Return
    A. Where you are now and what you are doing
    B. How you feel now and what you think of the stay in your host's home
    C. Concluding sentence — General statement of thanks, etc.

## Get-Well Note

A get-well note is a letter sent to a friend who is sick to cheer him up and let him know that you are concerned about him.

*Sample*
*(Get-Well Note)*

66 West Spring Street
Kansas City, MO 64111
October 29, 19 _____

Dear José,

    Miss Brown, our English teacher, has just told us that you were in the hospital for an appendectomy. I hope that you are feeling better now and that you will soon be completely recovered. Everyone in the class misses your good-natured personality and sense of humor. Besides, I have nobody to help me with my homework when you are away. We are all looking forward to your quick return. Please get well soon.

    With kindest regards and best wishes for your good health, I am

Your classmate,
Yasua

*Exercise*

Write a get-well note to a friend who is in the hospital with pneumonia. Be sure your note is cheerful.

# Spelling

Spelling in English is difficult because English is not a phonetic language. Many words, however, follow certain rules in their spelling.

| Spelling Rules | Examples |
|---|---|
| 1. [iy]: Put an *i* before *e* except after *c* or when *e-i* sounds like *a* [e] as in n*ei*ghbor. | grief    niece ⎫ *but* ⎧ receive    weight    vein<br>believe    relief ⎭ ⎩ deceive    freight    neighbor<br>*Exceptions:*<br>seize    either    neither    foreign<br>weird    leisure    height |
| 2. a. Words ending in silent *e* (lik*e*, tak*e*), drop the *e* before adding a suffix beginning with a vowel letter. | take — taking    ride — riding<br>bake — baking    fame — famous<br>dance — dancing    die — dying<br>*Exceptions:*<br>dye — dyeing    canoe — canoeing<br>shoe — shoeing    hoe — hoeing |
| b. Words ending in *ce* or *ge* generally keep the *e* before the suffix *able* or *ous*. (The *e* is needed to keep the "soft" sound of the *c* and *g* in these words.) | change — changeable<br>service — serviceable<br>outrage — outrageous |
| 3. Words ending in silent *e* (like *base*), keep the *e* before adding a suffix beginning with a consonant. | base — basement    safe — safety, safely<br>amuse — amusement    nice — nicely<br>rare — rarely<br>*Exceptions:*<br>argue — argument    whole — wholly<br>true — truly<br>*Note:* The words *judgement* and *judgment* are both correct. The same is true of *acknowledgement* and *acknowledgment*. |
| 4. Words ending in *y* preceded by a consonant, change the *y* to *i* before adding a suffix that does not begin with *i*. | marry — married, marriage ⎫ *but* ⎧ marrying<br>carry — carried, carriage ⎭ ⎩ carrying<br>angry — angrily |
| 5. a. Words of one syllable ending in a single consonant preceded by a single vowel, double the consonant before adding a suffix beginning with a vowel. | run — runner, running<br>fat — fatter<br>sit — sitter, sitting |
| b. Don't double the final consonant when there are two final consonants. | test — testing, tested<br>lock — locked, locking |
| c. Don't double the final consonant when two vowels precede the final consonant. | look — looking<br>break — breaking<br>heat — heating, heated |

| Spelling Rules | Examples |
|---|---|
| 6. a. When a word is accented on the last syllable and ends in a single consonant preceded by a single vowel (like be*gin*), double the final consonant before adding a suffix beginning with a vowel. | refer — referred, referring<br>begin — beginning<br>transfer — transferred, transferring<br>admit — admitted, admitting |
| b. Don't double the final consonant when the accent is on the first syllable. | travel — traveled, traveling |
| c. Don't double the final consonant when two consonants come at the end of the word. | resist — resisted, resisting |

# Plurals of Nouns

| Rules for Plurals of Nouns | Examples |
|---|---|
| 1. Most nouns form their plural by adding *s* to the singular form. | door — doors   table — tables<br>boy — boys   desk — desks |
| 2. Nouns ending in *s, ss, sh, ch, x,* or *z* form their plural by adding *es.* | dish — dishes   box — boxes<br>watch — watches   fizz — fizzes<br>church — churches   kiss — kisses<br>Jones — Joneses   atlas — atlases |
| 3. a. Nouns ending in *y* preceded by a consonant are made plural by changing the *y* to *i* and adding *es.*<br><br>b. *Nouns ending in y* preceded by a vowel are made plural by adding *s* only. | lady — ladies   try — tries   sky — skies<br>family — families   baby — babies   ally — allies<br>*Exception:* The names of people<br>Kelly — the Kellys<br>boy — boys   play — plays<br>key — keys |
| 4. Many nouns ending in *f* or *fe* change the *f* to *v* and add *es.* | wife — wives   life — lives   thief — thieves<br>shelf — shelves   leaf — leaves   calf — calves<br>*Exceptions:*<br>chief — chiefs   chef — chefs<br>handkerchief — handkerchiefs   roof — roofs<br>belief — beliefs   cliff — cliffs |
| 5. a. Nouns ending in *o* preceded by a vowel adds *s* to the singular.<br>b. Nouns ending in *o* preceded by a consonant usually add *es* to the singular. | rodeo — rodeos  patio — patios<br>shampoo — shampoos  audio — audios  zoo — zoos<br>tomato — tomatoes   hero — heroes<br>Negro — Negroes   echo — echoes<br>*Exceptions:*<br>banjo — banjos   piano — pianos<br>auto — autos   solo — solos |
| 6. Some nouns form their plural irregularly. | child — children   tooth — teeth   mouse — mice<br>man — men   foot — feet   louse — lice<br>woman — women   goose — geese   ox — oxen |
| 7. Some nouns have the same form in the singular and the plural. | sheep — sheep  fowl — fowl   Swiss — Swiss<br>deer — deer   Chinese — Chinese<br>fish — fish   Japanese — Japanese |

| Rules for Plurals of Nouns | Examples |
|---|---|
| 8. Compound nouns usually are made plural by adding *s* to the important word. | son-in-law — sons-in-law<br>passer-by — passers-by<br>high school — high schools<br>court martial — courts martial<br>*Exceptions:* When a compound word is written as one word the plural *s* is added to the whole word.<br>spoonful — spoonfuls    mouthful — mouthfuls<br>cupful — cupfuls |
| 9. Some nouns ending in *s* are usually singular. They have no plural form. | mumps        economics<br>measles      politics<br>news          mathematics |
| 10. Some nouns ending in *s* are always plural. They have no singular form. | scissors      pliers          pants<br>clothes       trousers      spectacles (glasses) |
| 11. Letters, numbers, and signs usually add *'s* to form the plural. | +'s      His *1*'s look like my *7*'s.<br>—'s      He minds his *p*'s and *q*'s.<br>          He never remembers to cross his *t*'s. |

# Capitalization

| Rules for Capitalization | Examples |
|---|---|
| **1. Capitalizing First Words** | |
|   a. Capitalize the first word of every sentence. | Where are you going? <br> My name is Anna. <br> How cold I am! <br> That boy can't speak Italian. |
|   b. Capitalize the first word of a direct quotation. | "Why were you late?" asked the teacher. <br> The student answered, "My car broke down." |
|   c. Capitalize the first word of a line of poetry. | 'Tis said that absence conquers love; <br>   But oh believe it not! |
|   d. Capitalize the first word of the greeting and all following nouns in a letter. | Dear Mr. Brown    Dear Sir <br> Gentlemen |
|   e. Capitalize the first word of the complimentary closing in a letter. | Sincerely yours,    Yours truly, <br> Very truly yours, |
| **2. Capitalizing Names of Persons** | |
|   a. Capitalize a person's given name or names and his family name. | Mary Brown    John Doe    Igor Bilbinski |
|   b. Capitalize all abbreviations used with a person's name, including his initials. | Prof. Watson         Mr. James A. Smith, Jr. <br> Dr. Freud <br> Gen. D. D. Eisenhower |
|   c. Capitalize titles of respect when they are used before a person's name. | President Johnson    General Bradley <br> Queen Victoria    Sir Winston Churchill <br> Professor Brown    Father O'Mally |
|   d. Capitalize words that show relationship, such as mother and father, when they are used in place of a person's name. | No, Dad, I didn't take your newspaper. <br> Yes, Mother, I'll be home by twelve. <br> We visited Grandma last Sunday. <br> I went to the park with Father. |
|   e. Don't capitalize a noun that shows relationship when there is a possessive pronoun before it, unless it is used with a person's name. | I wish my mother and father were with me now. <br> I saw my uncle last night. <br>   *But* — <br> My Uncle Willie travels a great deal. |
|   f. The pronoun *I* is always capitalized. | John and I are studying Spanish. <br> My husband and I went skiing last winter. |
| **3. Capitalizing Place Names** | |
|   a. Capitalize the names of definite geographic areas or divisions of the earth's surface. | the Orient    the West Coast <br> the Arctic Circle    the Temperate Zone |
|   b. The words north, south, east, and west are capitalized when they indicate parts of the world or parts of the country. When they indicate a simple direction, they are not capitalized. | Park Avenue is east of Broadway. <br> We spent our vacation in the West. <br> *Note:* The articles (a, an, the), the conjunctions (and, but, or) and short prepositions (at, on, by, etc.) are not capitalized unless used as the first word of a name or a title. |

| Rules for Capitalization | Examples |
|---|---|
| c. Capitalize the names of rivers, oceans, lakes, islands, and mountains. | Staten Island   Mt. Whitney   Lake Como<br>Atlantic Ocean   Amazon River   the Andes |
| d. Capitalize the names of countries, states, cities, towns, streets, and rural routes. | England   Route 1   Wall Street<br>Maine   Las Vegas   Fifth Avenue<br>Italy<br>the Dominican Republic |
| e. Capitalize the names of parks, buildings, and stations. | Grand Central Station   Chrysler Building<br>Empire State Building   Central Park |
| **4. Capitalizing Titles**<br>a. Capitalize the first word and each important word in the titles of books, magazines, newspapers, stories, articles, poems, and chapters of books. | The New York Times<br>Playboy<br>The Old Man and the Sea<br>Chapter 2: "The Rules of Grammar"<br>"How to Build a Bookcase"<br>*Note:* The articles (a, an, the), the conjunctions (and, but, or) and short prepositions (at, on, by, to, etc.) are not capitalized unless used as the first word of a name or title. |
| b. Capitalize the first word and each important word in the titles of plays, motion pictures, and radio and television programs. | Death of a Salesman   Dallas<br>My Fair Lady   Mission Impossible<br>Tarzan and the Apes |
| c. Capitalize each important word in the titles of famous documents. | the Magna Carta<br>the Constitution of the United States<br>the Declaration of Independence |
| **5. Capitalizing Religious Terms**<br>a. Capitalize all names referring to God or Jesus. | Allah   Zeus   Christ<br>Buddha   Jehovah   the Lord<br>Our Heavenly Father |
| b. The pronouns he, his, him, thou, they, and thine are capitalized when they refer to the Deity. | Trust in God, for He will lead you. |
| c. Capitalize all names for the Bible, its books and divisions, and names of other sacred books. | the Koran   Book of Genesis<br>the Talmud   the Old Testament<br>              the Good Book |
| d. Capitalize the names of religious bodies and their place of worship. | Catholic   Jewish   Protestant<br>Buddhist   Moslem   St. Patrick's Cathedral<br>                  First Presbyterian<br>                  Church |

| Rules for Capitalization | Examples |
|---|---|
| **6. Capitalizing Expressions of Time**<br>  a. Capitalize the names of the days of the week and the names of the months of the year. | Saturday    June<br>Sunday     July<br>Monday    November |
|   b. Don't capitalize the names of the seasons. | spring    fall    winter    summer |
|   c. Capitalize the names of holidays and the names of special occasions | Independence Day    Labor Day<br>Christmas     Ramadan |
|   d. Capitalize the names of historical periods and events. | the Renaissance    War of the Roses<br>the Dark Ages    First Crusade |
| **7. Capitalizing Names of Racial Groups, Nationalities, and Languages**<br>  a. Capitalize the names of racial groups. | Black    Caucasian    Asian |
|   b. Capitalize the names of nationalities. | Spanish    Australian    Swiss<br>French    Lebanese    Swedish |
|   c. Capitalize the names of languages. | Italian    Turkish    English<br>Chinese    Russian |
|   d. Capitalize adjectives derived from the names of racial groups, nationalities, and languages. | a Japanese camera    Thai silk<br>an English terrier    a French cook |
| **8. Capitalizing Trade Names, Names of Organizations, and Transportation**<br>  a. Capitalize the names of organizations and clubs. | Girl Scouts<br>International Student Association<br>Young Men's Christian Association |
|   b. Capitalize the names of business firms and the trade names of their products. | Ford Motor Company    General Motors<br>Pepperidge Farm Bread    Beechnut Gum<br>Cadillac<br>Thunderbird |
|   c. Capitalize the names of schools and other institutions. | American Language Institute<br>Boston University<br>Memorial Hospital |
|   d. Capitalize the names of departments and agencies of the Federal Government and of state governments. | Department of State<br>Bureau of Motor Vehicles<br>Department of Health and Human Services |
|   e. Capitalize the names of political parties. | Republican Party<br>Democratic Party<br>Socialist Party |
|   f. Capitalize the names of particular ships, trains, and airplanes. | The Chicago Limited    The Olympia<br>the Orient Express    the Eagle |
| **9. Additional Rules of Capitalization**<br>  a. School subjects are not capitalized unless they are names of languages or of specific numbered courses. | She is studying Spanish and chemistry this term.<br>Mr. Welles is teaching Chemistry I this term. |
|   b. O and oh. The formal interjection "O," used in direct address, is always capitalized. The interjection "oh" is not capitalized unless it begins a sentence. | Oh, did you want this seat?<br>He spent all his money, and oh, how sorry he was.<br>Where O where has my little dog gone? |

# Punctuation

It is important to use the correct punctuation marks in order to make your writing easy to understand. The correct use of punctuation marks helps make the written language clear and precise.

| Punctuation Mark | Use | Examples |
|---|---|---|
| The Period ( . ) | a. Use a period after a declarative or an imperative sentence. | I often watch television in the evening.<br>Give me the past tense of "speak."<br>We don't go to school on Saturday.<br>*The teacher said, "I want you to come early to class."<br>*Note: A period coming at the end of a quotation is generally placed inside the quotation marks. |
| | b. Use a period after most abbreviations. | Mrs.    Mr.    U.S.A.    etc.<br>Ave.    St.<br>Note: Periods are not used after the letters which represent longer names of trade organizations, government agencies, or international bodies.<br>YMCA    UNICEF    UN    NATO |
| | c. Use a period after an initial in a name. | H. G. Wells        Mrs. P. L. Maguire<br>John F. Kennedy |
| | d. Use a period between dollars and cents when the dollar sign is used. | $4.87    $.99    $123.45 |
| | e. Use a period before decimals or between the whole number and the decimal. | .74    .003    1.2    22.66    4.75 |
| The Question Mark ( ? ) | Use a question mark at the end of a direct question. (Note that question marks come only at the end of a sentence in English.) | How do you feel today?<br>Where are you going?<br>*The child asked his mother, "What time is Father coming home?"<br>† What did they do when you said, "I want to leave"?<br>Note:<br>    *A question mark goes inside the quotation mark when the quotation is a question.<br>    † If the complete sentence is a question, then the question mark goes outside the quotation marks. |
| The Exclamation Point ( ! ) | a. Use an exclamation point after an exclamatory sentence. | What a beautiful baby you have!<br>How nice of you to invite me! |
| | b. Use an exclamation point after a word, phrase, or sentence when you want to be very emphatic. | Hey! Look out! There's a car coming.<br>Ouch! You hurt my finger.<br>Why don't you keep quiet! |
| | c. Use an exclamation point to express emphatic commands. | Hurry up!<br>The policeman cried, "Stop thief!" |

| Punctuation Mark | Use | Examples |
|---|---|---|
| The Comma ( , ) | a. Use a comma after an introductory adverbial clause or verbal phrase. | If I don't learn English this semester, I will be very unhappy. (adverbial clause) |
| | | To learn a language, you must practice. (infinitive verbal phrase) |
| | | In talking to Jean about her plans, I found out that she was going to Hawaii. (gerund verbal phrase) |
| | | Disappointed in love, John started to drink. (participal verbal phrase) |
| | | *Exceptions:* |
| | | When the adverbial clause is short and closely related to the main clause, the comma may be omitted. |
| | | When we met we shook hands. |
| | | If I see Mary I will give her your message. |
| | b. Use a comma before a coordinating conjunction that joins the clauses of a compound sentence. The coordinating conjunctions are *and, but, or, nor, for, yet,* and *so.* | Your answers are correct, but you did the wrong exercise. |
| | | My alarm clock didn't ring this morning, and I was two hours late for work. |
| | | Don't walk out of the house without an umbrella, or you will surely catch a bad cold. |
| | | *Exceptions:* |
| | | When the two parts of a compound sentence are short, the comma may be omitted. |
| | | Jane danced and Robert sang. |
| | c. Use a comma to set off parenthetical and interrupting expressions. | Yes, Virginia, there is a Santa Claus. |
| | | Picasso's paintings are strange, aren't they? |
| | | My father, after all, is the head of the company. |
| | | Some Americans, however, use chopsticks when they eat Chinese food. |
| | d. A conjunctive adverb is often set off by a comma when it stands first in the clause. | Furthermore, I don't have enough money for the trip. |
| | | Accordingly, you will have to report to Dean Smith. |
| | e. Use a comma to set off a noun of address. | "Hugo, what time is it, please?" |
| | | "I'm sorry, Mr. Gomez, but Dr. Jones isn't in right now." |
| | f. Use a comma to set off an appositive. | Our new teacher, Mr. Green, comes from Illinois. |
| | | Miss Lark, our English teacher, comes from Maine. |

| Punctuation Mark | Use | Examples |
|---|---|---|
| | g. Use a comma to set off the second and all following items in a date or an address. | On January 1, 1863, Lincoln issued the Emancipation Proclamation.<br>The building at 33 West Street, Buffalo, New York, has been sold. |
| | h. Use a comma to separate items in a series. | My favorite sports are swimming, tennis, and skiing.<br>Tom eats breakfast at eight, lunch at noon, and dinner at seven.<br>*It was a warm, sunny, pleasant day.<br>*Note:* Since the three adjectives in this sentence are equal modifiers of *day,* they are separated by commas. When the last adjective in a series is thought of as part of the noun, no comma is used before it.<br>It was a warm spring day. |
| | i. Use a comma to set off non-restrictive phrases and clauses.<br>*Note:* Restrictive modifiers are those that are needed to get across the basic meaning of a sentence. They are *not* set off by commas.<br><br>Non-restrictive modifiers are not essential for the basic meaning of the sentence. They add details, helping to explain, illustrate, or describe; but the basic meaning of the sentence would be clear without them. They are always set off by commas. | The woman in the pink dress, who comes from Iowa, is a little deaf. (non-restrictive adjective clause)<br>The tiger, driven mad by hunger, killed the sheep. (non-restrictive participial phrase)<br>The students, under great pressure, took the examination. (non-restrictive prepositional phrase) |
| | j. Use a comma to set off a speaker's directly quoted words from the rest of the sentence. | Frank said, "I'll see you later."<br>"I'll see you later," Frank said.<br>"I'll see you later," Frank said, "back at the house." |
| | k. Use a comma for emphasis and contrast. | I want coffee, not tea.<br>It wasn't the children, but the adults, who were making all the noise. |
| | l. Use a comma to set off each group of three figures in a number over 999. | 12,444    3,480,753    1,000 |
| | m. Use a comma to set off degrees and titles. | James Kilroy, M.D.<br>John D. Rockefeller, Sr. |

| Punctuation Mark | Use | Examples |
| --- | --- | --- |
| Quotation Marks (" ") | a. Use quotation marks to enclose the exact words of a speaker. | The doctor said, "Bobby has a high temperature."<br>"I have just arrived," William said, "and I don't know anyone here."<br>"You shouldn't get out of bed," said the doctor. |
| | b. With direct quotations, marks of end punctuation are usually placed inside the quotation marks. | "Where are you going?" I asked my brother. |
| | c. Use quotation marks for titles of stories, articles, chapters, songs, and short poems. | The poem "Trees" was written by Joyce Kilmer.<br>Somerset Maugham wrote "A String of Beads." |
| | d. Quotation marks can be used to call attention to words that the writer is defining or explaining, and to special or technical terms that may be new to the reader. | It is customary to say "You're welcome" whenever anyone says "Thank you."<br>A "mugwump" is someone who sits on both sides of the fence at the same time. |
| The Colon ( : ) | a. Use a colon after the salutation in a business letter. | Dear Ms. Smith:    Gentlemen:<br>Dear Sir: |
| | b. In writing time, use a colon between the figure designating the hour and the figures designating the minutes. | I usually get up at 7:15 A.M. |
| | c. Use a colon after the expression *as follows* or *the following* to introduce a list. | The following languages are the official languages of the United Nations: English, French, Russian, Spanish, Chinese, and Arabic.<br>The names of the girls in the first row are as follows: Mary, Susan, Jane, Elsa, and Pamela. |
| The Semi-colon ( ; ) | a. Use a semi-colon between the two parts of a compound sentence if they are not joined by a coordinating conjunction. | The girls met in the auditorium; the boys met in the gymnasium.<br>Everyone laughed at his ideas; nevertheless, he kept on working. |
| | b. Use a semi-colon to separate items in a series if the items contain commas. | My classmates include Pierre, a Frenchman; Klaus, a German; and Yasuo, a Japanese. |
| The Hyphen ( - ) and the Dash ( — ) | a. Use a hyphen at the end of a line to indicate a divided word (broken into syllables). | Are you going to the reception tomorrow night? |

| Punctuation Mark | Use | Examples |
|---|---|---|
| | b. Use a hyphen to join words which are used as a single expression. | a two-year-old child    a two-cent stamp<br>a nine-year-old house<br>a five-story building<br><br>*Note:* In deciding whether to join two adjectives, try each one separately with the noun. If each can be used alone with the noun, no hyphen is needed. If either or both adjectives cannot be used alone, join them by a hyphen.<br>a big old tree   *but*   a brown-eyed girl |
| | c. Use a hyphen to connect compound numerals and fractions when they are written as words. | two-thirds        twenty-one<br>forty-second |
| | d. Use a dash to indicate a sudden change of thought. | I am going shopping today — but, perhaps, I will go tomorrow instead. |
| | e. Use one or two dashes to set off side remarks which could be left out without spoiling the sense of the sentence. | Buster — as everyone here calls him — is the best goalie in town.<br>My new dress — which my husband doesn't know about — costs a lot of money. |
| | f. Use a dash to separate two numbers referring to pages in a reference. | Gardner, Helen, *Art Through the Ages,* pages 94–96. |
| The Apostrophe ( ' ) | a. Use an apostrophe in a contraction to show the omission of one or more letters. | I won't go.<br>Where there's a will there's a way. |
| | b. Use an apostrophe to form the possessive case of a noun. | the girl's book      the students' desks |
| | c. Use an apostrophe to form the plurals of letters, numbers, and signs | 2's    x's    7's    #'s |
| Underlining ( __ ) | a. Use underlining to indicate the titles of books, magazines, newspapers, plays, radio and television programs, and motion pictures. | I read <u>The Grapes of Wrath</u> a long time ago.<br>I buy the <u>New Yorker</u> every week.<br>I saw that old movie <u>Perils of Pauline</u> on television. |
| | b. Use underlining for the names of a particular airplane, ship, or train. | The name of Lindbergh's plane was the <u>Spirit of St. Louis.</u><br><u>The Chicago Limited</u> is a fast train. |
| | c. Use underlining for words (or letters or numbers) used as words. | Be careful not to reverse the <u>e</u> and the <u>i</u> in <u>friend.</u> |

| Punctuation Mark | Use | Examples |
| --- | --- | --- |
| Parentheses ( ) | a. Use parentheses to enclose numbers or letters that mark the items in a series. | Before you mail the letter, be sure that you (a) seal the envelope, (b) put a stamp on the envelope, and (c) write your return address on the envelope. |
| | b. Use parentheses to put a side remark or a few extra words in a sentence that you think the reader will find helpful or interesting. | Ellen (standing in the corner with Bob) is the sister of my best friend. |

# Numbers

| Rules for Writing Numbers | Examples |
|---|---|
| 1. Numbers that can be expressed in one or two words are generally spelled out in ordinary writing; other numbers are usually written in figures.<br><br>    The form in which numbers are written should be consistent. If one of two or more numbers in a sentence cannot be expressed in two words or less, figures are used for all. | There were twenty-one people in the room.<br>Only two students came to class yesterday.<br>We passed 245 cars on the road yesterday.<br>Mr. Smith worked 160 hours last month.<br>There were 18 Frenchmen, 192 Americans, and 3 Chinese on the boat to Valparaiso. |
| 2. In business writing, figures are generally used since they usually express dimensions, weights, money, measure, totals, distances, etc., and it is easier to read figures. | 18 yards     3 by 5 inches<br>4 tons        5,000 miles<br>80%          $8.92 |
| 3. When a number occurs at the beginning of a sentence, it should be written out. | Fifty dollars isn't much to pay for that coat.<br>Ten percent of the people here speak Spanish. |
| 4. Figures are used for dates (except in very formal writing). | October 4, 1900   January 1st |
| 5. Figures are used for the time when A.M. or P.M. is used. | 4 P.M.   *but*   four o'clock |
| 6. Figures are used for street numbers (with no comma between thousands.) | 185 West End Avenue    1600 Broadway |
| 7. Figures are used for pages and other references. | p. 89   pp. 46-52   Chapter 14  *or*  Chapter XIV |
| 8. Figures are used for sums of money, except sums in round numbers or, in Formal Style, sums that can be written in two or three words. | $5.33   $.88   88¢<br>a million dollars  *or*  $1,000,000 |

# Division of Words

In English, if you must divide a word between two lines, you must break it between syllables and put a hyphen at the end of the first line. When you are not sure how to divide a word, look it up in a dictionary. English syllables are difficult to determine, but they usually follow pronunciation.

General rules to follow:

1. Words of one syllable are never divided.
2. Never divide a word so that a syllable of one letter stands alone.
3. Words that are spelled with a hyphen should be divided only at the point of the hyphen.

## A Good Rule to Follow

Try *not* to divide a word between two lines when you write a composition.

## QUIZ: LESSON 1

Fill in the blank spaces with the correct form of the verb *to be.*

*The Weather in Boston*

There _____ four seasons in Boston. The names of the seasons _____ winter, spring, summer, and autumn. In the winter it _____ often very cold and windy, and in the summer it _____ sometimes very hot and humid. The weather in the spring and autumn, however, _____ usually very pleasant. For many people these _____ the two best seasons of the year because they _____ the only times the climate _____ comfortable. There _____ one thing certain about Boston weather. It never stays the same. It changes every few hours.

## QUIZ: LESSON 2

### Quiz A

Fill in the blank spaces with the correct form of the verb *to be*.

*The Classroom*

Our English classroom _____ on the tenth floor of the Main

Building. It _____ a large room about twenty-five feet long and

eighteen feet wide. The walls _____ light green and tan, and

the ceiling is white. There _____ four windows on one side

of the room. Under the windows, there _____ two radiators

for heating the room in the wintertime. On the opposite wall, near

one end, there _____ a brown door, and next to it there _____

a thermostat. There _____ a large blackboard on the front wall

of the room with chalk and erasers on the ledge. The teacher's desk

_____ in front of this blackboard. In the back of the room, there

_____ a row of hooks on the wall for the students' coats and jackets.

There _____ about twenty light-colored chairs in the room for

the students. Each chair has a flat right arm. This arm _____ the

student's desk. On the whole, it _____ a pleasant and comfortable

room.

## Quiz B

Fill in the blank spaces with the correct expressions of place from the list below. Use each expression only once, and be sure to use the complete expression. Do not leave out any words!

*Expressions of Place*

on the front wall

on the ledge

in front of the blackboard

in the room

on the tenth floor

on one side

in the back of the room

next to it

on the opposite wall

under the windows

on the wall

*The Classroom*

The English classroom is _____ of the Main Building. It is a large room about twenty-five feet long and eighteen feet wide. The walls are light green and tan, and the ceiling is white. There are four windows _____ of the room. _____ _____ there are two painted radiators for heating the room in the wintertime. _____, near one end, there is a brown door, and _____ there is a thermostat. There is a large blackboard _____ of the room with chalk and erasers _____ . The teacher's desk is _____ . _____, there is a row of hooks _____ for the students' coats and jackets. There are about twenty light-colored chairs _____ for the students. Each chair has a flat right arm. This arm is the student's desk. On the whole, it is a pleasant and comfortable room.

## QUIZ: LESSON 3

Fill in the blank spaces with the correct form of the verb in parentheses.

*A Letter to a Friend*

Dear Mary,

   It _____ (be) three o'clock in the afternoon now, and I _____

(sit) in the library and _____ (write) you this letter. It is a

very pleasant, warm summer day and I _____

(look out) the window at Jefferson Park. There _____ (be) lots

of people in the park today. There _____ (be) many parents and

children in the playground. The children _____ (play) games

and _____ (chase) each other. The parents _____

(stand) or _____ (sit) in groups and _____

(talk) to each other. Some parents _____ (run

after) their children. There _____ (be) many elderly people in the park

today. Some _____ (read) newspapers, and some are just

resting on the benches. There _____ (be) also a lot of college students

in the park today. Some of the young men and women _____

(walk) in the park and _____ (hold) hands. (This isn't usual

in our country, but this custom is quite common here.) There _____

(be) lots of interesting people in the park today also, and I _____

(be) very busy people-watching. This _____ (be) one of my favorite

pastimes. It _____ (be) more interesting than doing homework.

However, I must say "Good-by" and get back to work.

Fondly,
Carla

## QUIZ: LESSON 4

### Quiz A

Fill in the blanks with the definite article, if necessary. If no article is necessary, put an X in the blank space.

*The United States*

_____ United States is a very large country. From the East Coast to the West Coast it is about 3,000 miles wide. _____ Atlantic Ocean is on the East Coast, and _____ Pacific Ocean is on the West Coast. _____ Canada is the country to the north of _____ United States, and _____ Mexico is the country to the south. _____ Rio Grande River is the boundary between Mexico and the United States. The major mountain ranges are _____ Appalachian Mountains in the East and _____ Rocky Mountains in the West. There are many rivers in the United States. The most important ones are _____ Mississippi and _____ Missouri Rivers in the central part of the country, and _____ Colorado and Columbia Rivers in the West.

The country is a composite of different geographic formations — high mountains and deep canyons, great river systems and landlocked lakes, rolling plains, forests and rocky coasts, sandy beaches, and even deserts. There are fifty states in the Union today. The two newest states, _____ Hawaii and _____ Alaska, are geographically separated from the other forty-eight states.

_____ United States is a heterogeneous country. The American people are of almost every race, every creed, and every nationality. This is because of the great immigration from abroad throughout American history. The population is now over 232 million people, including 1.3 million Native Americans. _____English is the common language.

## Quiz B

Fill in the blanks with the definite article, if necessary. If no article is necessary, put an X in the blank space.

*France*

_____ France is a republic on the continent of _____ Europe. The country borders on _____ English Channel, _____ Atlantic Ocean, _____ Spain, _____ Mediterranean Sea, _____ Italy, _____ Switzerland, _____ Luxembourg, and _____ Belgium. The capital city is _____ Paris. The most important rivers are _____ Loire, _____ Seine, and _____ Rhône. The major mountain ranges are _____ Pyrenees and _____ Alps. The population is over 46 million. The common language is _____ French.

## QUIZ: LESSON 5

### Quiz A

Rewrite the composition above the printed lines, and change the subject pronoun to *He*. Make all other necessary changes. All the italicized words require changes. Follow the example in the first sentence.

*What am I?*

_____
Mr. Dodd usually goes to work by subway.　　He

I usually go to work by subway.　　　　　　I *get* to work by 8:00 A.M.

_____

Before I *start* my job, I *put* on *my* uniform and *look* at *myself* in the mirror to

_____

*make* sure that I *look* neat.　　　　　At 8:30 in the morning, I *go* on duty.

_____

I usually *eat* lunch from twelve to one and generally *take* a fifteen-minute break in the

_____

morning and in the afternoon.　　　　At 4:30 in the afternoon, I *go* off duty.

_____

I *enjoy* my job very much.　　　　　I *meet* all kinds of people and talk to

_____

everyone.　　　　Many people ask *me* questions, and I *give* them the necessary

_____

information.　　　　I *try* to be very helpful.　　　　I always *call* out floors

_____

very clearly.　　　　I never *stay* in one place long.　　　　On the

_____

contrary, I *am* constantly on the move.　　　　Most men take off their hats in

_____

*my car*.　　　　Sometimes I *tell* passengers to put out their cigarettes.

_____

Some people smile at *me*, and others ignore *me*.　　　　*My* life is a series of

_____

"ups" and "downs."

## Quiz B

Fill in the blanks with the appropriate word.

*What is Mr. Dodd?*

Mr. Dodd usually goes to work _____ subway. He gets to work by 8:00 A.M. Before he starts his job, he puts _____ his uniform and looks _____ himself _____ the mirror to make sure that he looks neat. _____ 8:30 in the morning, he goes _____ duty. He usually eats lunch _____ twelve _____ one and generally takes a fifteen-minute break _____ the morning and _____ the afternoon. _____ 4:30 in the afternoon, he goes _____ duty.

He enjoys his job very much. He meets all kinds of people and talks to everyone. Many people ask him questions, and he gives them the necessary information. He tries to be very helpful. He always calls _____ floors very clearly. He never stays in one place long. _____ the contrary, he is constantly _____ the move. Most men take _____ their hats _____ his car. Sometimes he tells passengers to put _____ their cigarettes. Some people smile _____ him, and others ignore him. His life is a series _____ "ups" and "downs."

## QUIZ: LESSON 6

### Quiz A
Fill in the blanks with an appropriate contrasting adjective or noun.

*New York City*

   To most visitors, New York is both a fascinating and a _____

city. It is a city of great wealth and of great _____ . There

are many luxury apartment buildings, and there are many _____

tenements. There is a great deal of beauty and a great deal of _____ .

The parks and the shops are beautiful, but the dirty streets and the

subway stations are _____ . There are many tall skyscrapers

above ground and many winding subways _____ ground.

Most things are expensive, but some things are _____ . The

cost of entertainment is generally _____ , but there are

usually many free lectures, concerts, and art exhibits. There is an "_____

_____Side" and a "West Side" and an "_____" and a

"Downtown." There are people who work all _____ and

people who work all night. The city is never asleep. New York seems

unfriendly, but it really isn't.

## Quiz B

Fill in the blanks with the correct preposition.

*A Comparison of Two Cities (Shanghai and New York)*

Shanghai is different _____ New York _____ many

ways, but there are many things that are similar.

Shanghai is one _____ the most populated cities _____

Asia, and New York is one _____ the most populated cities _____

North America. The weather _____ the summer is very hot

_____ Shanghai, and it is the same _____ New York. Shanghai

is a port and an industrial city, and New York is too. Shanghai has a

problem _____ pollution, and New York has a similar problem. They

both have serious traffic problems.

The traffic problem _____ Shanghai is caused _____ too

many bicycles. The traffic problem _____ New York, _____ the

other hand, is caused _____ too many automobiles. The population

_____ Shanghai is homogeneous, but the population _____

York is heterogeneous. Most _____ the people _____

Shanghai live _____ apartments _____ low buildings, while

most _____ the people _____ New York live _____

apartments _____ high buildings. People eat _____ chopsticks

_____ Shanghai, but they eat _____ knives and forks _____

New York. While there are some differences, the major problems

_____ the big cities are almost the same everywhere _____

the world.

## QUIZ: LESSON 7

Fill in the blanks with the correct form of the verbs in parentheses.

*Political Speech*

   Fellow Chicagoans! This _____ *(be) your mayor speaking.*
*Chicago* _____ (face) a financial crisis. The city _____
(be) heavily in debt, and we _____ (have) to increase
taxes. We _____ (need) more money for low income
housing. We _____ (need) more money for the
city's schools. We _____ (need) more money for the transit
system and for the police department. I _____ (plan) to
ask the state and federal government to help us.

   Chicago _____ (be) a city divided racially now, and that cannot
be. I _____ (hope) to solve the problems of racial
division. I _____ (strive) for unity. Chicago _____
_____ (be) a united city. I _____ (intend) to
be the mayor of all Chicago. I _____ (want) to reach
out my hand in friendship and fellowship to everyone in this city. I _____
_____ (need) your help.

   It _____ (take) the cooperation of every Chicagoan.
Together, we _____ (solve) the city's problems. We
_____ (make) Chicago "the city that works."

# QUIZ: LESSON 9

## Quiz A

Rewrite the composition above the printed lines, and change the subject pronoun to *he*. Make all other necessary changes. All the italicized words require changes. Follow the example in the first sentence.

*A Typical Day*

> *The alarm clock rings at seven o'clock every morning, and John usually gets up at once.*

The alarm clock rings at seven o'clock every morning, and I usually get up at once.

---

*He*

*I jump* out of bed and *do* physical exercises for ten minutes.      Then I

---

*am* ready either to get back into bed or to take a quick cold shower.

---

After *my* shower, *I plug* in *my* electric razor and *shave.*

---

Then *I plug* in my electric toothbrush and *brush my* teeth.      Next,

---

*I comb my* hair, *wash my* face again, and *put on* after-shave lotion.

---

After that, *I pick out my* suit, shirt, and tie for that day.

---

*I get* dressed and then *I eat* breakfast.      For breakfast, *I usually*

---

*have* grapefruit juice, scrambled eggs, toast, and coffee.      After

---

breakfast, *I* sometimes *smoke* a cigarette and *listen* to the news on the radio.

---

At 8:00 A.M., *I put* on *my* coat and *I leave* for school.

---

*I* generally *go* to school by subway.      The subway is always crowded, and *I don't* often get a seat. In the subway, on *my* way to school, *I look*

at the signs on the walls of the car, *watch* the faces of the other passengers, and

*read* the newspaper headlines over someone's shoulder. It takes *me*

about half an hour to get to school. *My* first class begins at nine o'clock,

and *my* last class ends at three. After school hours, *I* sometimes *go*

to the Student Center or to a coffee house with *my* friends for an hour or so.

Afterwards, *I go* home.

As soon as *I get* home from school, *I sit* down and *do my* homework and *study*

*my* lessons for the next day. At seven o'clock *I eat* dinner with *my*

brother. Then *I relax.* Some nights *I watch* television

for an hour or two, *read,* or *write* letters. Other nights, *I listen* to

my jazz records or *work* on *my* stamp collection. Sometimes *I take*

a walk in the evening, or *visit* a friend, or *go* out on a date. *I* usually *get* home by

midnight because by twelve o'clock *I am* generally rather tired.

*I take* off *my* clothes, *get* into bed, and *fall* asleep immediately. *I sleep*

until the alarm clock goes off again the next morning.

## QUIZ: LESSON 9

### Quiz B

Fill in the blanks with the correct word.

*A Typical Day in My Life*

My alarm clock rings _____ seven o'clock every morning, and I usually get _____ at once. I jump _____ of bed and do physical exercises _____ ten minutes. Then I am ready either to get back _____ bed or to take a quick cold shower. _____ my shower, I plug _____ my electric razor and shave. Then I plug _____ my electric toothbrush and brush my teeth. Next, I comb my hair, wash my face again, and put _____ after-shave lotion. _____ that, I pick _____ my suit, shirt, and tie _____ that day. I get dressed and then I eat breakfast. _____ breakfast, I sometimes smoke a cigarette and listen _____ the news _____ the radio. _____ 8:00 A.M., I put _____ my coat and I leave _____ school.

I generally go _____ school _____ subway. The subway is always crowded, and I don't often get a seat. _____ the subway, _____ my way _____ school, I look _____ the signs _____ the walls of the car, watch the faces _____ the other passengers, and read the newspaper _____ someone's shoulder. It takes me _____ half an hour to get to school. My first class begins _____ nine o'clock, and my last class ends _____ three. _____ school hours, I sometimes go _____ the Student Center or _____ a coffee house _____ my friends _____ an hour or so. _____ , I go home.

As soon _____ I get home _____ school, I sit _____ and do my homework and study my lessons _____ the next day. _____ seven o'clock I eat dinner _____ my brother. Then I relax. Some nights I watch television _____ an hour or two, read, or write letters. Other nights I listen _____ my jazz records or work _____ my stamp collection. Sometimes I take a walk _____ the evening, or visit a friend, or go _____ on a date. I usually get home _____ midnight because _____ twelve o'clock I am generally rather tired. I take _____ my clothes, get _____ bed, and fall asleep immediately. I sleep _____ the alarm clock goes _____ again the next morning.

## QUIZ: LESSON 10

Fill in the blanks with the correct word.

*My Last Vacation*

Last summer I spent a two-week vacation _____ Miami Beach,

Florida. My roommate and I flew _____ Miami _____ New York

_____ three hours. It was the first time _____ both _____

us, and we went there because the rates are lower off-season. We

stayed _____ an air-conditioned luxury hotel _____ the beach.

Every morning we slept late and then had breakfast outdoors _____

the pool. When the weather wasn't too hot, we used to go sightseeing

_____ the morning. We visited the Seaquarium, the campus

of the University of Miami, and the Everglades. _____ the afternoon,

we used to go swimming _____ the ocean or the pool, lie _____

the sun, or go water-skiing. _____ dinner _____ the

evening, we used to go dancing _____ a discotheque or watch the

entertainment _____ the night clubs. The weather was very

good every day, and the two weeks went _____ too quickly. We were

both very sorry when the vacation ended.

## QUIZ: LESSON 11

### Quiz A
Fill in the blanks with a suitable adjective.

*My Classmate*

Mr. Sago is one of my classmates. He is a _____ man of

_____ height and build, and he is a little on the

_____ side. He has _____ hair that

is starting to get _____, a _____ face,

and a _____ complexion. His most outstanding feature is

his eyes. They are very _____ and _____,

with _____ lashes, and they seem to be smiling at you

all the time. This gives Mr. Sago the appearance of being very _____

_____ or of being up to some mischief. On the whole,

Mr. Sago is a _____ dresser, and he usually wears a

_____ suit. His ties, however, are _____.

He goes in for _____ prints in his ties. Mr. Sago speaks

very quickly but in a _____ voice. He has a _____

_____ wit and enjoys a _____ joke.

He is a very _____ student, but he doesn't always

pay attention in class. Sometimes he writes letters in class, and sometimes

he clicks his _____ pen or taps his pencil on the desk.

But he soon settles down to work again. He gets along with the other

students, and most of them like him very much.

## Quiz B

Fill in the blank spaces with an appropriate word.

*My Classmate*

Mr. Sago is one _____ my classmates. He is a young man _____ medium height and build, and he is a little _____ the chubby side. He has curly black hair that is starting to get thin, a round face _____ a small chin, and a fair complexion. His most outstanding feature is his eyes. They are very dark and alive, _____ long black lashes, and they seem to be smiling _____ you all the time. This gives Mr. Sago the appearance _____ being very good-natured or _____ being _____ to some mischief. _____ the whole, Mr. Sago is a conservative dresser, and he usually wears a gray or dark-blue suit. His ties, however, are wild. He goes _____ for loud-colors or abstract prints _____ his ties. Mr. Sago speaks very quickly but _____ a soft voice. He has a keen wit and enjoys a good joke. He is a very intelligent student, but he doesn't always pay attention _____ class. Sometimes he clicks his ballpoint pen or taps his pencil _____ the desk. But he soon settles _____ to work again. Mr. Sago gets along well _____ the other students, and most _____ them like him very much.

## QUIZ: LESSON 12

### Quiz A
Write the correct prepositions in the blank spaces.

*A Letter*

It has been a busy semester _____ me. Since my arrival, I have

gone _____ a tour _____ this city. I have been _____ the

top _____ the Washington Monument. I have seen some plays

and films _____ the Kennedy Center for Performing Arts. I have

eaten _____ many restaurants and tried different national dishes. I

have spent a lot of money _____ magazines, books, and art

reproductions.

I haven't gone _____ a symphony concert or _____ a ballet

performance yet. I haven't been _____ Arlington National Cemetery

or _____ a boat trip on the Potomac.

Last weekend, I visited Congress and sat _____ _____

one of the sessions. Next weekend, some of the other foreign students and

I are going to speak _____ a student group _____ one of the

suburbs. Then, we are going to have dinner _____ some American

families. I will tell you all about it _____ my next letter.

## QUIZ: LESSON 12

### Quiz B

Write the correct tense of the verb in parentheses.

*A Letter*

Dear Pablo,

I _____ (be) sorry I _____ (write — *negative*) you since I _____ (leave) home six months ago, but it _____ (be) a busy semester for me. In spite of my heavy work schedule, I _____ (manage) to have some fun.

Since my arrival, I _____ (go) on a tour of the city and _____ _____ (visit) some famous landmarks and tourist spots. I_____ _____ (take) some pictures to prove it, too. I _____ already _____ (visit) the Smithsonian Institution and the National Gallery of Art. I _____ (go) on a tour of the White House and _____ (see) where the President lives. I_____ _____ (be) to the top of the Washington Monument and _____ (visit) the Jefferson and Lincoln Memorials. My roommate and I _____ (see) some plays and films at the Kennedy Center for the Performing Arts. I_____ already_____ _____ (eat) in a Vietnamese, a Brazilian, and a Mexican restaurant and_____ (try) different national dishes. I_____ _____ (also _____ (spend) a lot of money on magazines, books, and art reproductions.

I still _____ (do — *negative*) everything I would like to do before I_____ (leave) this city. I_____ _____ (go — *negative*) to a symphony concert or to a ballet performance yet. So far, I _____ (be — *negative*) to Arlington National Cemetery or _____ (take) a boat trip on the Potomac River. However, I _____ (intend) to do all these things in the near future. I _____ (make — *negative*) any new friends up to now, but I _____ (hope) to meet some soon. The International Festival next month_____ _____ (be) a good time to do this.

Last weekend, I _____ (visit) the Capitol and _____ (sit) in on one of the sessions of the Senate, the upper house of Congress. It _____ (be) very interesting. Next weekend, some of the other foreign students and I _____ (speak) before a student group in one of the suburbs. Then we _____ (have) dinner with some American families. I _____ (tell) you all about it in my next letter. Please write soon and tell me what you have been doing.

Your friend,<br>Maria

## QUIZ: LESSON 13

Fill in the blanks with the correct form of the verb in parentheses.

*Bad Habits*

Everybody _____ (have) some personal habits that he or she

would like to get rid of, and I _____ (be) no exception.

_____ (eat) too much _____ (be) my number one

bad habit. This _____ (be) a difficult habit to break, and as

a result I _____ (be) always on a diet. _____ (twirl)

my hair _____ (be) another bad habit. Whenever I _____

_____ (be) nervous or uncomfortable, I _____

(fall back) into this childhood pattern, and whenever I _____

(be) very tired, I _____ (have) the bad habit of _____

(talk) too much and _____ (say) foolish things. This habit

_____ (be) something I always _____ (regret) the

next day.

Other people _____ (have) habits that I _____

(like — *negative*) either. Students who _____ (click) their

ballpoint pens in class _____ (drive) me up a wall. People who

_____ (move — *negative*) to the rear of a bus and who

_____ (block) the doors make me very angry. People who

_____ (put — *negative*) the cap back on a tube of toothpaste

are another pet peeve. I _____ (find) this habit very annoying.

Unfortunately, we all _____ (do) things unconsciously

that _____ (bother) other people, but that _____

(be) because nobody _____ (be) perfect.

## QUIZ: LESSON 14

Fill in the blanks with the correct words.

*How to Get Along in the United States*

Dear _____,

You have asked me _____ suggestions on how to get along

_____ the United States. It is difficult to give advice, but I have found

the following "do's" and "don'ts" helpful.

_____ a rule, it isn't easy to find anyone to talk to _____ a big

city. However, here are some suggestions. First, get or borrow a dog!

Walk him several times a day! Americans love pets and usually stop to talk

_____ anyone _____ a dog. Then, try to eat _____ a

cafeteria. People generally share the same tables and will sometimes talk to

you if they see that you are a stranger. Next, take your dirty clothes to a

laundromat! It takes about an hour to wash and dry laundry, and

many people wait _____ the laundromat. They often pass the time

talking _____ the other customers. Always ask _____

information _____ a woman, if you are a man, and _____ a

man, if you are a woman! It seems to get better results _____ a reason

I can't understand. Learn the expressions, "Please," "Thank you,"

and "You're welcome" _____ you come, and use them all the time!

They usually work _____ magic.

There are some things you shouldn't do. Don't tell the truth when people

ask "How are you?" They only expect the answer to be "Fine." Never

ask people their age — men or women. Everyone wants to be young. Don't

tell heavy people they are fat. Tell them they are losing weight. Everyone here is diet-conscious and wants to be thin. Don't be late _____

appointments! When someone says six o'clock, be sure to be there

_____ six. Americans respect time and expect everyone to be

"_____ time."

_____ all, don't worry! Just follow my advice and bring a lot

_____ money and you will get along. I hope I have been _____

some help _____ you.

Your friend,

Miguel

## QUIZ: LESSON 15

Fill in the blanks with the past tense of the verb in parentheses.

*An Unusual Dream*

 I don't dream very often, but when I do, I always have unusual dreams.
As a matter of fact, I had an extraordinary dream last week.

 It _____ (be) a beautiful day, and I _____
(be) on a big ship. The sea _____ (be) calm and quiet, the sky
blue and clear, and the sun warm and bright. Suddenly, heavy clouds
covered the sky. The sun disappeared, the wind _____ (begin)
to blow, and the sea turned to gray. There was such a fierce storm that
the ship almost _____ (sink). At that moment another
ship appeared from out of the dense fog. It was a pirate ship with a black
flag and a crew of armed pirates. The pirates jumped onto our ship, and the
battle _____ (begin). I was assailed by three pirates at
once. One pirate _____ (have) a long beard, the second
_____ (have) a black mustache, and the third _____
(have) a wooden leg. I _____ (have) a sword in my
hand, and I _____ (fight) bravely. All around me a violent
battle raged. Soon I was wounded and _____ (lie) bleeding
on the deck. Then, all at once, a very beautiful girl appeared on the
other ship. She _____ (give) some sharp commands, and
all the pirates disappeared. Their ship seemed to have been gulped down.
Immediately the storm stopped and the sun _____ (come
out) again. I was dazzled.

 Just then I _____ (awake) and _____ (find) that
I was in my own bed. The sun was shining, and there _____ (be)
a ray of light on my face. Perhaps it _____ (be) that sunbeam
that had changed my nightmare into a dream of adventure.

## QUIZ: LESSON 16

### Quiz A
Fill in the blanks with the correct tense of the verb in parentheses.

*My First Day in the United States*

   I _____ (arrive) in the United States on February 5, 1983, but I _____ (remember) my first day here very clearly. My friend _____ (wait) for me when my plane _____ (land) at Kennedy Airport at three o'clock in the afternoon. The weather _____ (be) cold and it _____ (snow), but I _____ (be) too excited to mind. From the airport, my friend and I _____ (take) a taxi to my hotel. On the way, I _____ (see) the skyline of Manhattan for the first time, and I _____ (stare) in astonishment at the famous skyscrapers and their man-made beauty. My friend _____ (help) me unpack at the hotel and then _____ (leave) me because he _____ _____ (have to) go back to work. He _____ (promise) to return the next day.

   Shortly after my friend _____ (leave), I _____ _____ (go) to a restaurant near the hotel to get something to eat. Because I couldn't _____ (speak) a word of English, I couldn't tell the waiter what I _____ (want). I _____ (be) very upset and _____ (start) to make some gestures, but the waiter _____ (understand — *negative*) me. Finally, I _____ (order) the same thing that the man at the next table _____ (eat). After dinner, I _____ (start) to walk along Broadway until I _____ (come) to Times Square with its movie theaters, neon lights, and huge crowds of people. I _____ (feel — negative) tired, so I _____ (continue) to walk around the city. I _____ (want) to see everything on my first day. I _____ (know) it _____ (be) impossible, but I _____ (want) to try.

When I _____ (return) to the hotel, I _____
_____ (be) exhausted, but I couldn't sleep because
I _____ (keep) hearing the fire and police sirens during
the night. I _____ (lie) awake and _____
(think) about New York. It _____ (be) a very big and
interesting city with many tall buildings and big cars, and full of noise and
busy people. I also _____ (decide) right then that I
_____ (have to) learn to speak English.

## QUIZ: LESSON 16

### Quiz B

Fill in the blanks with the correct prepositions.

*My First Day in the United States*

    I arrived _____ the United States _____ February 5, 1983, but I remember my first day here very clearly. My friend was waiting _____ me when my plane landed _____ Kennedy Airport _____ _____ three o'clock _____ the afternoon. The weather was very cold and it was snowing, but I was too excited to mind. _____ the airport, my friend and I took a taxi _____ the hotel. _____ the way, I saw the skyline _____ Manhattan _____ the first time, and I stared _____ astonishment _____ the famous skyscrapers and their man-made beauty. My friend helped me unpack _____ the hotel and then left me because he had to go back _____ work. He promised to return the next day.

    Shortly _____ my friend had left, I went _____ a restaurant _____ the hotel to get something to eat. Because I couldn't speak a word _____ English, I couldn't tell the waiter what I wanted. I was very upset and started to make some gestures, but the waiter didn't understand me. Finally, I ordered the same thing that the man _____ the next table was eating. _____ dinner, I started to walk _____ Broadway until I came _____ Times Square _____ its movie theaters, neon lights, and huge crowds _____ people. I didn't feel tired, so I continued to walk _____ the city. I wanted to see everything on my first day. I knew it was impossible, but I wanted to try.

    When I returned _____ the hotel, I was exhausted, but I couldn't sleep because I kept hearing the fire and police sirens _____ the night.

I lay awake and thought _____ New York. It was a very big and interesting city _____ many tall buildings and big cars, and full _____ noise and busy people. I also decided right then that I had to learn to speak English.

## QUIZ: LESSON 17

### Quiz A
Fill in the blanks with the correct form of the verb in parentheses.

*A National Holiday*

Thanksgiving Day is always celebrated on the fourth Thursday of November. It _____ (be) the most traditional of American holidays. The first Thanksgiving was held in Massachusetts in 1621. After a year of great hardship, the Pilgrim colonists _____ (want) _____ (give) thanks to God for their first harvest. They _____ (invite) their Indian friends _____ (join) them in a big feast. Today the holiday is still celebrated as a day for giving thanks. It _____ (be) a day of family reunion, and it _____ (be) customary _____ (invite) friends _____ (share) the meal. In some large cities, there _____ _____ (be) carnival parades for children. In other cities, there _____ (be) important football games that are played on Thanksgiving Day.

In my family, we always _____ (go) to my grandmother's house on Thanksgiving Day. All my aunts, uncles, cousins, nephews, and nieces _____ (gather) for a family homecoming. We always _____ (invite) some friends _____ (join) us. Everyone _____ (be) glad _____ (see) everyone else and there _____ (be) a very busy exchange of gossip. Some of us soon _____ (disappear) into the kitchen _____ (help) my grandmother _____ (prepare) the dinner. Others, meanwhile, _____ (settle down) _____ (watch) a football game on television or to discuss business or politics. If the weather _____ (permit), some of the more athletic of us _____ (go) outside _____ (play) ball with the children. At about four o'clock, we all _____ (sit down) to dinner. My grandfather _____ (give) thanks for the blessings we _____ (receive), and then he _____ _____ (start) _____ (carve) the turkey. We always _____ (have) the traditional dinner of stuffed turkey, cranberry sauce, apple cider, sweet potatoes, chestnuts, and pumpkin pie. After dinner, no one can move, and we all _____ (sit around) and _____ (talk), play word games, or tell jokes until it _____ (be) time _____ (go) home. It _____ (be) always difficult _____ (leave) because Thanksgiving Day _____ (be) one of the few days of the year when the entire family _____ (get together).

## QUIZ: LESSON 17

### Quiz B
Fill in the blank spaces with the correct words.

*A National Holiday*

Thanksgiving Day is always celebrated _____ the fourth Thursday _____ November. It is the most traditional _____ American holidays. The first Thanksgiving was held _____ Massachusetts _____ 1621. _____ a year of great hardship, the Pilgrim colonists wanted to give thanks _____ God _____ their first harvest. They invited their Indian friends to join them _____ a big feast. Today the holiday is still celebrated as a day _____ giving thanks. It is a day _____ family reunion, and it is customary to invite friends to share the meal. _____ some large cities, there are carnival parades _____ children. _____ other cities, there are important football games that are played _____ Thanksgiving Day.

_____ my family, we always go _____ my grandmother's house _____ Thanksgiving Day. All my aunts, uncles, cousins, nephews, and nieces gather _____ a family homecoming. We always invite some friends to join us. Everyone is glad to see everyone else, and there is a very busy exchange _____ gossip. Some of us soon disappear _____ the kitchen to help my grandmother prepare the dinner. Others, meanwhile, settle _____ to watch a football game _____ television or to discuss business or politics. If the weather permits, some _____ the more athletic of us go outside to play ball _____ the children. _____ about four o'clock, we all sit _____ to dinner. My grandfather gives thanks _____ the blessings we have received, and then he starts to carve the turkey. We always have the traditional dinner _____ stuffed turkey, cranberry sauce, apple cider, sweet potatoes, chestnuts, and pumpkin pie. _____ dinner, no one can move, and we all sit _____ and talk, play word games, or tell jokes until it is time to go home. It is always difficult to leave because Thanksgiving Day is one _____ the few days _____ the year when the entire family gets together.

## QUIZ: LESSON 18

Fill in the blanks with the correct form of the verb in parentheses.

*An Important Object*

When I _____ (be) a child I _____ (have)
many toys, but the thing I _____ (remember) best _____
_____ (be) three yards of gold-colored silk. This _____
_____ (be) my favorite plaything. My father _____
(bring) it home one day, along with many other things, after one of his
trips abroad. When he _____ (ask) me what I _____
(want), I _____ (choose) this piece of silk. Not only _____
_____ (be) it beautiful to look at, but it _____
(be) also soft and smooth to touch. The three yards of gold silk and I soon
_____ (become) inseparable. It _____ (be)
my passport into the world of fantasy. With it, I could _____
(become) any character I _____ (read) or _____
(hear) about by draping and twisting the silk into different costumes. One
day I _____ (be) Cinderella all dressed up for the ball;
another day I _____ (be) Little Red (Gold) Riding Hood;
and still another day I _____ (be) Wonder Woman or someone
from another planet. Sometimes I _____ (be) a bride or a
princess, and other times I _____ (be) a ballet dancer or
a famous actress. I _____ (be) an Indian woman in a sari, a
South Sea Islander, and once even an Eskimo. I _____
(be) anybody I _____ (want) to be.

Today, I can still _____ (remember) the wonderful
sense of escape that it _____ (give) me. All my childhood
toys and games _____ (be) long since gone, but somewhere in
a box at the bottom of a closet there _____ (be) still three
yards of gold-colored silk.

# QUIZ: LESSON 19

## Quiz A

Fill in the blanks with the correct comparative form of the adjectives and adverbs in parentheses.

*Two Friends*

Human beings are social animals, and it is in their nature to form friendships. People are very lucky if, among their friends, they have one really close and intimate friend. I have two such friends. Their names are George and Kevin. They both have brown hair and brown eyes, and they both have gentle personalities. George is two years _____

_____ (old) Kevin and _____

(tall) and _____ (thin). He is built _____

_____ (straight) as an arrow, and his face is

_____ (long) and _____

(angular) Kevin's. Kevin is _____ (short) but

_____ (strong) George and has a _____

_____ (full) and _____

(round) face. Kevin is _____ (quiet) George

and talks much _____ (little) George does. George

is _____ (cheerful) Kevin and always tells us

jokes and funny stories about his life. He is _____

(experienced) in life than Kevin because he has lived a _____

_____ (adventurous) life. George is also

_____ (impatient) Kevin. George is accustomed

to doing everything quickly, from working to talking. Kevin, on the

other hand, speaks and works much _____

(slowly). Both of them respect time and are usually early for an appointment.

## Quiz B

Fill in the blanks with the correct verb form.

*Two Friends*

Both Kevin and George like nature and outdoor sports and are fond

of _____ (hike), _____ (swim), and _____

_____ (jog). They are both interested in music but George

_____ (prefer) country western and rock, while Kevin would

rather _____ (listen) to classical music. In reading, their

tastes _____ (be) similar and they both _____

(enjoy) _____ (read) biographies and books about

history. They _____ (be) both career-oriented, but George

_____ (want) _____ (be) a fashion designer while

Kevin _____ (want) _____ (be) a computer

programmer. At times their personalities _____ (seem)

very different, but at other times they _____ (seem) very much

alike. I _____ (feel) very fortunate all the time, however,

to have them both as friends.

## QUIZ: LESSON 20

Fill in the blanks with the correct preposition.

*Marriage*

Americans seem to be going back _____ the patterns _____ their great-grandparents, postponing marriage _____ favor _____ an education and a career. Back _____ the early 1900's, men and women both married _____ older ages. Then there followed a period when they married younger and younger. According _____ a survey taken _____ March 1982, the typical American male was 25.2 years old _____ getting married _____ the first time. _____ women, the median age was 22.5 _____ a first marriage. Not _____ 1910 had men waited that long to marry. Women hadn't delayed marriage _____ that age _____ this century.

While both men and women are marrying later _____ life, the number _____ unmarried-couple households has more than quadrupled _____ 1970. That, however, is still only 4 percent _____ all couples.

## QUIZ: LESSON 21

Fill in the blanks with the correct form of the verb in parentheses.

*The Ideal Teacher*

The ideal teacher may _____ (be) young or old, tall
or short, fat or thin. She should _____ (know) her
subject, but she can _____ (make) mistakes if she
_____ (be) willing to learn. Her personality _____
_____ (be) as important as her scholarship. The
ideal teacher must _____ (be) enthusiastic. She must
never _____ (teach) anything she _____
_____ (be) not interested in. She should _____
_____ (be) a bit of an actress, and she shouldn't
_____ (be) afraid to show her feelings and _____
_____ (express) her likes and dislikes. She must
_____ (like) her students and _____
(respect) them, but she must also _____ (respect)
herself and _____ (take) pride in her work. Otherwise,
she cannot _____ (respect) her students. The ideal
teacher should _____ (have) an understanding of her
students and _____ (be) able to relate to them. She
should _____ (be) kind, encouraging, and helpful, and she
should _____ (motivate) her students to want to
learn. The ideal teacher should _____ (see) her students
as individuals and _____ (acknowledge) their differences.
She must _____ (know) how to encourage the

self-development and growth of each of her students. The ideal teacher

_____ (be) one who _____ (grow),

_____ (learn), and _____ (improve)

herself along with her students.

## QUIZ: LESSON 22

Fill in the blank spaces with the correct voice and tense of the verb in parentheses:

*My First Flight*

Last summer, I _____ (take) my first airplane

flight from Zurich to Chicago. I _____ (board) the

plane at Kloten Airport and, from that moment on, my life _____

_____ (arrange) for me on the trip. First, I

_____ (direct) to my seat by the flight attendant.

Then, when the plane _____ (be) ready to take off,

the other passengers and I _____ (tell) to fasten

our seat belts. A few minutes after take-off, magazines and newspapers

_____ (pass out). Because my ears hurt, I _____

_____ (give) some gum to chew. Next, the

passengers _____ (give) instructions on what to

do in case of an emergency. We _____ (give)

earphones to listen to music and _____ (tell) that a

movie _____ (show) after dinner. Before dinner,

we _____ (ask) if we _____

(want) a cocktail. Dinner _____ (serve) on a tray,

but it _____ (be) attractive and delicious. We

_____ (permit) to have a refill on any beverage.

After dinner, we _____ (show) a new Hollywood

movie. When I _____ (feel) cold, I _____

_____ (give) a blanket and when I felt airsick,

I _____ (give) a paper bag. Everything _____

_____ (do) for the comfort of the passengers.

When the plane _____ (land), I _____

_____(be) almost sorry to get off and have

to start _____ (do) things for myself again.

## QUIZ: LESSON 23

### Quiz A
Fill in the blanks with the past tense of the verb in parentheses.

*Abraham Lincoln*

Abraham Lincoln _____ (be) born in a log cabin in Kentucky on February 12, 1809. When he _____ (be) a small boy, his family moved to the frontier of Indiana. Here, his mother _____ (teach) him to read and write. Lincoln _____ (have) very little formal education, but he _____ (become) one of the best-educated men of the Great West.

When Lincoln _____ (be) a young man, his family moved to the new state of Illinois. Lincoln _____ (have to) earn a living at an early age, but in his leisure time he _____ (study) law. He soon _____ (become) one of the best-known lawyers in the state capital, Springfield, Illinois. It _____ (be) here that Lincoln _____ (become) famous for his debates with Stephen A. Douglas on the subject of slavery.

In 1860, Lincoln was elected President of the United States. He _____ (be) the candidate of the new Republican Party. This party opposed the creation of new slave states. Soon after Lincoln's election, some of the Southern states _____ (withdraw) from the Union and _____ (set up) the Confederate States of America. This action _____ (bring on) the terrible Civil War which lasted from 1861 to 1865.

On January 1, 1863, during the war, Lincoln issued his famous Emancipation Proclamation. In this document, Lincoln proclaimed that all the slaves in the seceding states were to be set free as of that date. In 1865, after the war ended, the Thirteenth Amendment was added to the Constitution of the United States. This amendment _____ (put) an end to slavery everywhere in the United States.

Early in 1865, the Civil War _____ (come) to an end with the defeat of the South by the North. Only a few days after the end of the war, Lincoln was shot by an actor named John Wilkes Booth. The President _____ (die) on April 14, 1865. In his death, the world _____ (lose) one of the greatest men of all time.

## Quiz B

Fill in the blanks with the correct word.

*Abraham Lincoln*

Abraham Lincoln was born _____ a log cabin _____ Kentucky _____ February 12, 1809. When he was a small boy, his family moved _____ the frontier of Indiana. Here, his mother taught him to read and write. Lincoln had very little formal education but he became one _____ the best-educated men _____ the Great West.

When Lincoln was a young man, his family moved _____ the new state _____ Illinois. Lincoln had to earn a living _____ an early age, but _____ his leisure time he studied law. He soon became one _____ the best-known lawyers _____ the state capital, Springfield, Illinois. It was here that Lincoln became famous _____ his debates _____ Stephen A. Douglas _____ the subject of slavery.

_____ 1860, Lincoln was elected President _____ the United States. He was the candidate _____ the new Republican Party. This party opposed the creation _____ new slave states. Soon _____ Lincoln's election, some _____ the Southern states withdrew _____ the Union and set _____ the Confederate States of America. This action brought _____ the terrible Civil War which lasted _____ 1861 _____ 1865.

_____ January 1, 1863, during the war, Lincoln issued his famous Emancipation Proclamation. _____ this document, Lincoln proclaimed that all the slaves in the seceding states were to be set free as _____ that date. _____ 1865, after the war ended, the Thirteenth Amendment was added _____ the Constitution _____ the United States. This amendment put an end _____ slavery everywhere _____ the United States.

Early _____ 1865, the Civil War came _____ an end with the defeat _____ the South _____ the North. Only a few days _____ the end _____ the war, Lincoln was shot _____ an actor named John Wilkes Booth. The President died _____ April 14, 1865. _____ his death, the world lost one _____ the greatest men _____ all time.

## QUIZ: LESSON 24

Fill in the blanks with the correct tense of the verbs.

*A Reported Conversation*

Last night, John _____ (dream) that he

_____ (meet) Columbus and that they _____

_____ (have) a conversation.

John asked Columbus what he _____ (do)

now, and Columbus answered that he _____ still

_____ (look) for a shorter route to India. Then

John asked him what _____ (happen) to the land

he _____ (discover) in 1492. Columbus replied

that he _____ (think) it _____

_____ (become) a country full of automobiles and

television sets. Next, John asked him what the name of the country

_____ (be) now, and Columbus said that he

_____ (think) it _____

(call) the United States of America. John then asked Columbus if many of his

men _____ (get) seasick coming over to the

New World, and Columbus replied that he _____

(know — negative) what the word _____

(mean). John told him that it _____ (be — negative)

important. Then, John asked Columbus if he _____

(think) he _____ (return) to the country he

_____ (discover). Columbus replied that

he _____ (think — *negative*) so because the people

_____ (speak) English there now, and he couldn't

understand the language.

## QUIZ: LESSON 25

Fill in the blank spaces with the correct preposition.

*The American Family*

The most common type _____ family _____ the United

States is the nuclear family. The nuclear family is typically made up

_____ two generations — parents and their still-dependent children.

The typical family is middle-class, and there is usually some kind _____

equality _____ the husband and the wife. Each family lives

_____ its own separate residence, and it is not usual to share a house

_____ one's grandparents or in-laws. American families are very

mobile and are continually changing jobs and moving _____ other

neighborhoods. It is estimated that an average family moves _____

once every five years. The care of children _____ an American

family is exclusively the responsibility _____ their parents, and

children are taught to be independent _____ an early age. Adult

children usually leave their parents' house and set _____ their own

households even though they are not married.

The American family is undergoing real change. _____ example,

American families have fewer children today and some choose to have

none. _____ addition, more mothers are working due _____ a

combination _____ economic reasons and the changing social

climate. Divorce is quite common, and one _____ the most disturbing

changes is that millions _____ children are being brought up

_____ one parent, usually the mother. Nevertheless, most divorced

people remarry, and many _____ these remarriages include a

child _____ a former marriage. Therefore, there are many new

patterns _____ family life emerging _____ the United States.

## QUIZ: LESSON 26

Fill in the blanks with the correct word.

*Time Capsule*

If I were asked to select five items to represent American life today

that would be placed _____ a 3′ × 3′ × 3′ time capsule not to be

opened _____ the year 5000, I would choose the following items. The

first item would be a pair _____ jogging shoes. This would represent

the American people's craze _____ physical fitness _____

present. Next, I would include a picture _____ a hamburger and

_____ a roadside MacDonald's or Burger King. Fast food chains are

proliferating all _____ the country, and the pictures would represent

an American food habit. The third item would be a computer. We are

living _____ a computer age today, and it is predicted that every

child will soon become familiar _____ the computer _____

school, and that every business and most homes will soon have one as well.

The fourth item would be the book, *How to Live to be 100 — or more,* by George

Burns. This is advertised as "the ultimate diet, sex, and exercise book"

and would be an example of the kind of book that always appears

on America's best-seller lists. The last item would be a videotape _____

a few soap operas. On this one could see the clothes _____ today,

the homes _____ today, and some _____ the problems

Americans face _____ their social life. When they open the capsule

in the year 5000, I wonder what the people of the future will think

_____ us.

## QUIZ: LESSON 27

### Quiz A
Fill in the blanks with the correct form of the verb in parentheses.

*American Humor*

American humor _____ (be) difficult to define because Americans _____ (be) such a diverse people. In the early days, when the country _____ (be) largely agricultural, America's humor _____ (derive) from stories about people in the rural areas. Then, as the country _____ (develop) and _____ (become) more urban and industrialized, there _____ (be) many jokes contrasting the sophistication of the city dweller and the naiveté of the country folk. Here _____ (be) an example of one such joke.

An artist driving through a rural area _____ (see) a quaint rustic with a picturesque mountain in the background.

"I _____ (give) you twenty dollars if you _____ (let) me _____ (paint) you," he _____ (say).

The mountaineer _____ (keep) chewing his tobacco in silence as he _____ (think) it over.

"You wouldn't have to do anything for the money," the artist _____ _____ (add), trying to persuade him.

"I _____ (think — negative) about the money, _____ (say) the rustic, "I _____ (wonder) how I'd get the paint off when you are finished."

Today, American humor _____ (adapt) and _____ (restyle) to reflect the new conditions of present day life. The following _____ (be) an example.

As the airplane _____ (take off) from O'Hare Airport, a metallic voice _____ (come) over the loudspeaker: "Ladies and gentlemen, Vista Airlines would like _____ (welcome) you to the first translantic flight that _____ _____ (control) completely by computer. The possibility of human error _____ (eliminate) because there _____ (be) no pilot and no crew aboard. All of your needs _____ (take care) of by the very latest technology. Just _____ (relax) and _____ (enjoy) your flight. Every contingency _____ (prepare) for, and nothing can possibly go wrong . . . go wrong . . . go wrong."

A good appreciation of humor _____ (be) healthy both for a country and an individual. People _____ (laugh) at different things, but if you can _____ (laugh) at yourself, then you _____ (have) a truly mature sense of humor.

## QUIZ: LESSON 27

### Quiz B

Fill in the blank spaces with the correct word.

*American Humor*

American humor is difficult to define because Americans are such a diverse people. _____ the early days, when the country was largely agricultural, America's humor derived _____ stories _____ people _____ the rural areas. Then, as the country developed and became more urban and industrialized, there were many jokes contrasting the sophistication _____ the city dweller and the naiveté _____ the country folk. Here is an example _____ one such joke.

An artist driving through a rural area saw a quaint rustic _____ a picturesque mountain _____ the background.

"I'll give you twenty dollars if you let me paint you," he said.

The mountaineer kept chewing his tobacco _____ silence as he thought it _____.

"You wouldn't have to do anything _____ the money," the artist added, trying to persuade him.

"I'm not thinking _____ the money," said the rustic, "I was just wondering how I'd get the paint _____ when you're finished."

Today, American humor has been adapted and restyled to reflect the new conditions of present day life. The following is an example.

As the airplane took _____ from O'Hare Airport, a metallic voice came _____ the loudspeaker: "Ladies and gentlemen, Vista Airlines would like to welcome you _____ the first transatlantic flight that is being controlled completely _____ computer. The possibility _____ human error has been eliminated because there is no pilot and no crew aboard. All _____ your needs will be taken care _____ by the very latest technology. Just relax and enjoy your flight. Every contingency has been prepared _____, and nothing can possibly go wrong . . . go wrong . . . go wrong."

A good appreciation _____ humor is healthy both _____ a country and an individual. People laugh _____ different things, but if you can laugh _____ yourself, then you have a truly mature sense _____ humor.